The Battle over Marriage

The Battle over Marriage

Gay Rights Activism through the Media

LEIGH MOSCOWITZ

University of Illinois Press

URBANA, CHICAGO, AND SPRINGFIELD

Library of Congress Cataloging-in-Publication Data
Moscowitz, Leigh.
The battle over marriage : gay rights activism through the media /
Leigh Moscowitz.
    pages   cm
Includes bibliographical references and index.
ISBN 978-0-252-03812-9 (hardcover : alk. paper) —
ISBN 978-0-252-07960-3 (paperback : alk. paper) —
ISBN 978-0-252-09538-2 (e-book)
1. Same-sex marriage—Press coverage—United States. 2. Gay rights—
Press coverage—United States. 3. Gays in mass media. I. Title.
HQ1034.U5M67   2013
306.84'80973—dc23   2013015221

For Amelia and Eli

Contents

Acknowledgments

As with any large-scale research project, I am indebted to many individuals whose support, insights, and guidance made this book possible, from its inception to its completion. First and foremost, I am indebted to and inspired by my activist informants—the communications directors, public relations directors, and presidents and founders of many of the nation's leading gay rights organizations. These are people who work long hours for their cause and their community and yet still gave their time to me. In their offices, in coffee shops, and in gay bars, they shared with me stories of their own coming out, what it was like to see their lives reflected in the media and popular culture, and how their views about marriage changed when they began planning their own commitment ceremonies and weddings. Their perspectives transformed this project and the ways in which I will approach my research in the future.

I am also incredibly appreciative of the careful and attentive work of the anonymous reviewers of this manuscript. The time and attention they devoted to reading, commenting on, and critiquing an earlier version of this book shaped my thinking about this project. Their insights proved invaluable as I continued to refine my arguments. This book would not have been possible without the guidance, feedback, and support of my editor, Danny Nasset, at the University of Illinois Press, and the work of the production team. I am also indebted to my father-in-law, Ray Moscowitz, who put his editorial expertise to work in meticulously fine-line editing each chapter across a period of months. I am grateful for his countless hours of unpaid labor, thoughtful questions, and the journalistic lens he provided my work.

I also want to thank my fantastic colleagues at the College of Charleston, who made it fun to come to work every day. They have created a truly enjoyable and collegial place to work, full of positive energy and encouragement. I am grateful for my department chairs, Brian McGee and Bethany Goodier, who wrote supportive letters and assisted in procuring funding for the project, and for the mentorship of Alison Piepmeier, who helped me navigate through the world of academic publishing.

This book began nearly a decade ago at the Indiana University School of Journalism, and I will forever be indebted to my "Dream Team" committee, Professors Elizabeth Armstrong, Betsi Grabe, Dave Weaver, and my chair, Radhika Parameswaran. This group of mentors provided me with foundational tools throughout my research training—the tools to think, to write, and to ask interesting questions. Most important, they instilled in me a passion for academic work. Their own scholarship guided and inspired this project. They dedicated countless hours to advising, counseling, and meticulously editing drafts. I am endlessly grateful to Radhika, whose belief in the project—and in me as the one to do it—meant I could not waver. I am also indebted to the many other scholars whose work laid the foundation for this project, specifically the work of Edward Alwood, Larry Gross, and Suzanna Walters, to name a few.

I thank the Association for Education in Journalism and Mass Communication (AEJMC) for their continued support of this project, first for recognizing this work as the winner of the Nafziger-White-Salwen Dissertation Award and later as an AEJMC Scholars grant recipient. I knew I had hit the jackpot when Carolyn Kitch agreed to be my mentor for the AEJMC Scholars program; her insights and feedback on my proposal and on chapter drafts helped me take this project to the next level. This work also received financial awards from Indiana University and the College of Charleston. These student and faculty research and development grants made it possible for me to travel and interview activists face-to-face and assisted in the purchasing of videotaped news programs from the Vanderbilt Television News Archive.

As fantastic as the journey is, the process of beginning a new life as an academic comes with a unique set of challenges. In particular, writing a book, at various points in the process, feels self-indulgent, unrealistic, and entirely out of reach. It was the love of friends and family members from all across the country that sustained me. I am indebted to Mary-Tina Vrehas, whose friendship and persistent optimism have been a bedrock of strength for me, and to Tamara Leech, whose balance of scholarship, activism, and parenting is inspirational. I am grateful for the encouragement of colleagues and friends—people like Andy Billings, April Bisner, Jeff Bennett, Erin Benson,

Janis Cakars, Melissa Cakars, Spring Duvall, Suz Enck, Lori Henson, Claire King, Mike Lee, David Parisi, Kristin Swenson, Brynnar Swenson, Darrel Wanzer, Isaac West, the "sandwich" colleagues at Butler University, and many others.

I am indebted to my parents—my father, James Stickler, who through his own model ultimately inspired me to be a teacher and an academic, and to my mother, Beverly Mehrlich, whose belief, strength, and tireless counseling provided me the emotional support to see it through. The support of my family members has been a constant—people like Rick Mehrlich, Christy and Mike Conway, Erica and Chip Gray, and John and Stephanie Stickler. Ray and Barbara Moscowitz provided endless support, encouragement, and, as previously noted, editorial expertise.

Finally, there is nothing that makes you analyze your own relationship like writing a book about marriage. And so I owe the greatest debt to my partner of the last twenty-plus years, David Moscowitz, a man who infuses everything in his life—his scholarship, his teaching, his children, even his beloved pets—with the sort of vitality and optimism that stirs you. He did all the little things to keep me going, whether it was taking the kids to the park, bringing me coffee, or staying up with me into the morning hours so I could finish a chapter.

David also gave me the children I thought I could never have, children who continue to amaze me and frustrate me and delight me throughout this process. My children and this project literally grew together; Amelia (now nearly ten) was a year old when I began to study media coverage of same-sex marriage, and Elijah (now seven) was born soon after the first period of interviews. My project is marked by them, both literally and figuratively. I remember Amelia scribbling on my coding sheets, helping me "fill them out," and Eli, scrunched a little too tightly inside my protruding stomach, kicking me incessantly as I interviewed informants. This book is ultimately for Amelia and Eli, in the hope that they will grow up in a culture where they can be who they choose to be and love whom they choose to love.

The Battle over Marriage

1. Gay Marriage in an Era of Media Visibility

> My marriage, it's my center. It's the core of who I am as a human being. It's the base that you turn back to.
>
> —Carol Adair, who married her lesbian partner
>   of 25 years in San Francisco in February 2004

> There are millions of Americans angry and disgusted by what they see on TV—two brides, two grooms, but not a man and a woman. This is the new civil war in America.
>
> —Randy Thomasson, executive director
>   of the Campaign for California Families

For nearly a decade, longtime partners Davina Kotulski and Molly McKay celebrated Valentine's Day by dressing up in traditional wedding garb: Davina in a tux, Molly in a white gown. They stood in line with hundreds of opposite-sex couples at San Francisco's city hall to request a marriage license. Every year, they were denied one. As a committed lesbian couple and activists in the movement for marriage equality, Davina and Molly rehearsed their annual futile quest for a marriage license precisely so that they would be turned down in front of local television news crews and newspaper photographers. With the goal of creating, as Davina put it, "a media stir," they came year after year to protest their exclusion to the institution of marriage, to "render visible the discrimination we face on a daily basis."

On February 16, 2004, Davina and Molly's desire for a state-sanctioned wedding was finally fulfilled. Capturing headlines around the globe, San Francisco mayor Gavin Newsom had begun issuing marriage licenses to same-sex couples in defiance of California law. Approximately 1,400 gay and lesbian couples, many of whom had traveled hundreds of miles to wait in line overnight in the cold rain, met in San Francisco to be a part of the media-dubbed same-sex "marriage marathon." Millions of Americans who tuned in to national and local television news broadcasts witnessed something they had not seen before, which for most was beyond their imagination: gay and lesbian couples getting married "legally"—at least what was considered

SAN FRANCISCO, CA: San Francisco sheriff's deputies place handcuffs on same-sex couple Molly McKay (right) and Davina Kotulski (left), longtime activists in the marriage equality movement, after they staged a sit-in protest on February 14, 2011. Close to a dozen same-sex couples who were denied marriage licenses were arrested after the demonstration inside the office of San Francisco's county clerk. (Photo by Justin Sullivan/Getty Images)

temporarily legal. By the end of the week, more than 3,900 gay and lesbian couples were married.

The matrimonial marathon that took place in San Francisco was one of the most visible moments in a series of legal and cultural events that catapulted the issue of gay marriage to the center stage of mainstream cultural debate.[1] In the 2000s same-sex marriage emerged not only as an important election year issue but also as a central battle waged in the culture wars. Homosexuals' bid for marriage rights quickly became a wedge issue, "one of the cultural fault lines dividing the two Americas" in what was already a contentious political climate (Rosenberg & Breslau, 2004, p. 23).

Moreover, the intense news coverage of the divisive issue in the U.S. media focused unprecedented attention on gay and lesbian life. Stories like those of Davina and Molly were featured in national newsmagazines and on morning news programs. The topic of gay marriage became a front-page story in leading national newspapers like the *Washington Post* and the *New York Times*. Local papers across the country, especially in conservative regions, gave the issue "dramatic play" (Jurkowitz, 2004, p. 1). Images of same-sex couples waiting in line to obtain marriage licenses led the local and evening newscasts. Almost overnight, as *USA Today* reported, gay marriage replaced abortion as "the most volatile social issue" in the 2004 presidential election (Page, 2003). As lead anchor Tom Brokaw proclaimed to television news audiences on *NBC Nightly News,* "Never have the words 'I do' been so divisive" (Reiss, 2004, May 16).

Today, of course, these stories and images of same-sex nuptials are almost passé. By 2013 thirteen states and the District of Columbia had legalized marriage for same-sex couples, and think tanks and media outlets alike showed a sea-change in growing public support. In 2008 a *Newsweek* poll declared a "gay marriage surge," and surveys from the Pew Research Center showed that by 2012 more American adults favored same-sex marriage (48 percent) than opposed it (43 percent) (Pew Forum, 2012). That figure represents a 17 percent increase from 2004, when only 31 percent supported gay marriage and nearly twice as many Americans opposed it (Pew Research Center, 2012).

This shift in increasing public support for gay marriage is perhaps most visible in the arena of electoral politics. In 2004 the George W. Bush reelection campaign ran on, and many would argue won on, an anti–gay marriage platform. Eight years later, in a televised interview that attracted worldwide news attention, President Barack Obama told ABC's Robin Roberts that same-sex marriage should be legal. A mere four years earlier, support for gay marriage on the national stage was the equivalent of campaign suicide—a politically volatile hot potato that no candidate wanted to touch. During the 2012 election season, however, gay marriage headlined at the Democratic National Convention, the first time ever that the issue of marriage equality was introduced in a major party platform. While pundits and strategists questioned the Obama camp's motives during this election season, no one could ignore how the center of gravity on the issue had shifted. As Geoff Garin, a Democratic pollster, told the *New York Times,* "The majority of voters are comfortable with the position Obama has taken on [same-sex marriage]. The issue is a defining one for younger voters, who see it as a litmus test of whether someone is in sync with modern times and their generation" (Baker, 2012).

But on the issue of same-sex-marriage rights, contradictions abound. President Obama's personal proclamation for marriage equality came the day after voters in North Carolina—also the site of the Democratic National Convention—passed an initiative to ban same-sex marriages (even though gay marriage was already illegal in the state). Consistently, gay marriage measures have been defeated at the ballot box, losing in total 32 statewide referenda that have gone up for public vote. It wasn't until November 2012 that voters approved gay marriage rights through the electoral process, making same-sex marriages legal in Maryland, Maine, and Washington State.

To date, battles continue over the legality of California's Proposition 8 ("Prop 8"), which in 2008 outlawed same-sex marriages, a crushing defeat for the gay rights movement. After a dizzying number of legal twists and turns, in August 2010 U.S. District Court Judge Vaughn Walker struck down the California voter initiative as unconstitutional, legalizing gay marriages in the state once again. Prop 8 proponents appealed the decision, and the case now awaits hearing by the U.S. Supreme Court.

This book is concerned with the media coverage that helped to define and shape one of the most contentious social issues of the last decade, the same-sex-marriage debate. Through an analysis of media reports and in-depth interviews with leaders of the modern gay rights movement, *The Battle over Marriage* offers a critical and longitudinal examination of how media frames and activist discourses evolved surrounding this definitive civil rights issue. My focus is from 2003 to 2010, a period of intense media scrutiny, legal activity, shifting public opinion, and evolving political discourses.

This study interrogates the aims and challenges of leading gay rights activists who sought to harness the power of mainstream news media to "change hearts and minds"—to advocate for their cause and reform images of their community. In doing so, I join an evolving academic and popular conversation about how news coverage frames contemporary social issues and movements. This book also speaks to a growing body of work on the emergence of gays and lesbians in the media and popular culture, using news narratives and representations as a critical but under-studied source of information about gay and lesbian life.

Who was granted a voice in mainstream media debates on this controversial civil rights issue? How did gay and lesbian rights groups attempt to shape coverage of the debate? What images and narratives about gay and lesbian life did activists foreground? What were the dominant journalistic devices—including frames, sources, and visual images—that media storytellers relied upon to produce this story for news audiences? And in what ways did the media attention surrounding the marriage issue reshape the structure, organization, and goals of the contemporary gay rights movement? These are the central questions I am concerned with in this book. To investigate these concerns, I conducted 30 in-depth interviews with the nation's leading gay rights activists at two different time periods in this debate—in 2005 and again in 2010—in order to reveal the behind-the-scenes goals, strategies, and struggles of social movement actors who worked within the confines of commercial news media to "sell" gay marriage to a largely unreceptive

American public. I also conducted qualitative and quantitative analyses of a broad range of news media texts throughout this time period, including prominent, large-circulation newsmagazines; national newspapers in print and online; national network television news broadcasts; and prime-time television news programs. Ultimately this project shows the complex ways that media coverage of the gay marriage debate both aided and undermined the cause, revealing both the progressive potential and the limitations of commercial media as a route to social change.

*   *   *

Before I identify the major intellectual frameworks for the study of gay marriage in the news and why they matter, I want to return to the story of Molly and Davina. For them, a couple who had celebrated their union in a commitment ceremony with family and friends six years earlier, the experience of being "backed by the law" at San Francisco's city hall in 2004 was transformative. Davina explained to me the cultural significance of marriage as society's "shorthand for who gets what and who is related to whom."

On that day in 2004, Molly and Davina also became national media spokespersons. The traditional act of sealing the ceremony with a passionate kiss was captured by videographers, newspaper photojournalists, and magazine photographers. Molly and Davina's climactic kiss of conjugal bliss morphed into an iconic symbol for the gay marriage movement, appearing in regional newspapers like the *San Francisco Chronicle*; in national publications like *Newsweek, Time,* and *USA Today*; in two documentary films; and on several television news programs.

This couple's story points to the two central concerns of this book. First, I am interested in how activists like Molly and Davina talk of marriage, a historically exclusionary institution, as a route to inclusive citizenship and cultural acceptance. The media landscape has been an important site of struggle for challenging and (re)defining marriage, an institution imbued with cultural meanings and social significance that are largely taken for granted. Defining marriage in particular ways legitimizes some individuals and relationships by prohibiting others. Because marriage is irrevocably tied to citizenship and nationhood, the gay marriage debate is not only about homosexuals' bid for marriage rights but also about how we define ourselves as a culture and a nation. Narratives of gender, race, sexuality, nationhood, and family are intertwined with news discourses about same-sex marriage.

Second, Molly and Davina's story highlights how the gay marriage debate became largely a *mediated* issue in public discourse—an issue we learn about and experience through newspapers, magazines, television news programs, and web stories. Coverage of same-sex marriage in mainstream news connects with larger theoretical concerns about how social movements gain access to the media and the politics of media representations.

To understand the significance of stories like Molly and Davina's, and the process by which these stories become media spectacles, it is first necessary to position media coverage of the gay marriage controversy within several larger intellectual frameworks in the fields of media studies and queer studies. To begin this discussion, I briefly outline the major legal and political developments in the United States that catapulted gay marriage onto the front pages of prominent national newspapers and magazines. Next I highlight why this study is important by connecting my work to the major bodies of scholarship on the visibility of gay and lesbian people in the news and popular culture; the complicated interdependent relationship between social movements and media; and the role of marriage as a political and social institution. Finally, I briefly explain how I selected the news stories and activists for this study, and I outline the plan of the book.

Same-Sex Marriage: Legal and Political Contexts

The evolution of the gay marriage debate in the United States has many different histories with multiple beginning points. In subsequent chapters I reflect more on the origins of the debate, especially from the perspectives of gay rights activists, some of whom have been fighting for marriage equality since the early 1980s. For my purposes here, I focus on the central events that piqued the public interest beginning in the mid-1990s and culminated in the explosion of media attention in the early to mid-2000s.

The fight for marriage equality in the United States has evolved on a state-by-state level, with early activity focused on Hawaii. A great deal of public attention centered on the 1996 Hawaii court case in which it was ruled that banning same-sex couples from participating in marriage was unconstitutional. The lower court sent the controversial case back to the state's supreme court. Fearing that Hawaii would become the first state to legalize same-sex unions, Congress passed a federal act in 1996 dubbed the Defense of Marriage Act (DOMA). Signed into law by President Bill Clinton, this act defined for the first time on a federal level the term "marriage" as between one man and one woman and the term "spouse" as someone of the opposite sex. DOMA also gave states the right to refuse to recognize same-sex marriages performed in other states.

In 2000 the issue once again made headlines when Vermont became the first state to offer civil unions that legally recognize same-sex couples. These civil union arrangements provide gay couples some, though not all, of the rights and protections that marriage affords heterosexual couples. Vermont's then governor, Howard Dean, signed the civil union bill into law. These early steps in Hawaii and Vermont paved the way for the contemporary controversy over gay marriage in the 2000s, the time period that is the central concern of this study.

Beginning in the summer of 2003, a series of legal and political events pushed gay marriage to the forefront of mainstream politics. In June 2003 Ontario, Canada, legalized marriage for same-sex couples, opening the door to thousands of Canadian couples, as well as American couples who crossed the border, to marry without restrictions. That same month, the U.S. Supreme Court ruled in *Lawrence v. Texas* that all 13 remaining state sodomy laws were unconstitutional. Considered a landmark case for gay civil rights, conservative judges and activists warned that the ruling would open the door to the legalization of same-sex marriage (see chapter 3 for a discussion of this case).

At the state level, gay rights activists and same-sex couples who wanted to marry legally challenged state-level DOMA legislation. Activists argued that to deny gays and lesbians marriage rights under the law was discriminatory and unconstitutional. In November 2003 the Massachusetts Supreme Judicial Court ruled on behalf of seven plaintiff couples in *Goodridge et al. v. Department of Public Health,* arguing that the state constitution mandates that same-sex couples should have access to civil marriage. Three months later, in February 2004, the Massachusetts court clarified its earlier decision in *Goodridge* and ruled that anything less than marriage—including civil union arrangements—fails to provide equal protections for same-sex couples and is therefore unconstitutional under the law.

That same month, as detailed earlier in this chapter, San Francisco mayor Gavin Newsom defied California law and issued same-sex marriage licenses to more than 3,900 gay and lesbian couples. Newsom told *Nightline's* Ted Koppel that his motivation to issue the licenses was to end what he saw was a discriminatory practice in the state of California, and also in part as a retaliatory response to the Bush administration's political agenda. As he explained on *Nightline,* Newsom was emphatic that buried in the president's 2004 State of the Union Address was a thinly disguised attempt to amend the Constitution in order to ban same-sex marriages. "It was crystal clear to me, and I imagine the tens of millions of Americans that were watching [the State of the Union], that this was a political strategy for the White House to play some divide and conquer strategy to placate their right, in an effort to advance a political agenda . . . The president, he can fly on some aircraft carrier any time he wants, but he should keep his hands off the Constitution" (Sievers, 2004, February 24).

In the days and weeks that followed, several other cities like Portland, Oregon, and New Paltz, New York, began issuing licenses to same-sex couples. Immediately, President George W. Bush publicly announced his support for the Federal Marriage Amendment that would make same-sex marriages in any state illegal and unconstitutional. Echoing concerns from his conservative base, he said that in the wake of the Massachusetts and San Francisco decisions, "activist judges" and local authorities had too much power to redefine "the most fundamental institution of civilization" (Sievers, 2004, February 24). Since the Constitution was first ratified, it has been amended 27 times, the first 10 of these making up the Bill of Rights. Thus, President Bush argued before Congress that the matter of gay marriage had risen to the level of constitutional concern: "If we are to prevent the meaning of marriage from being changed forever, our nation must enact a constitutional amendment."

Three months after their decision to make same-sex marriages constitutional, on May 17, 2004, the state supreme court denied a last-minute appeal and Massachusetts became the first state to issue state-sanctioned same-sex marriage licenses (DePasquale, 2004). In front of television cameras and newspaper reporters, all seven plaintiff couples from the *Goodridge* case married that day. The historic moment in the movement for marriage equality drew attention from media outlets throughout the country and around the globe (the "I do" heard around the world), as "the dramatic cultural milestone generated headlines and commentary everywhere from Rio de Janeiro to Prague" (Jurkowitz, 2004, p. 1). The director of *Newseum,* a website that posts the front pages of 300 newspapers on a daily basis, proclaimed that the same-sex-marriage case in Massachusetts "is what we call an 'A story day'" (Jurkowitz, 2004, p. 1).

Nevertheless, the successful "cultural milestone" that gay rights activists had achieved in the courts did not appear to hold up in the court of public opinion. The day gay and lesbian couples were first married in Massachusetts, anti–gay marriage protesters chanted, "We'll remember in November." On Election Day, November 2004, they held true to their promise. The intense campaigning efforts of gay marriage opponent groups like the Defense of Marriage Coalition, the Family Research Council, and the Christian Coalition, resulted in ballot initiatives in 11 states to ban same-sex marriages. Many political analysts argued that the issue of gay marriage "was a key part of Karl Rove's turnout strategy," bringing social conservatives supporting George W. Bush to the polls in record numbers (Rosenberg & Breslau, 2004, p. 23). By comfortable margins, all 11 states—including Arkansas, Georgia, Kentucky, Michigan, Mississippi, Montana, North Dakota, Oklahoma, Ohio, Utah, and Oregon—voted to prohibit same-sex marriages. In some states, including

Ohio, Michigan, and Utah, anti-marriage groups successfully pushed measures that not only banned gay marriage but also repealed domestic partnership benefits that even affected unmarried heterosexual couples (Rosenberg & Breslau, 2004).

These losses prompted some of the more prominent gay rights organizations that had lobbied for same-sex marriage to rethink their political strategy and moderate their goals (Broder, 2004; Lester, 2004). As Matt Foreman, then director of the National Gay and Lesbian Task Force (commonly known as the Task Force), said, "There now is a profound realization that this struggle is going to go on for a very long time" (Lester, 2004). The Human Rights Campaign announced they would recruit more non-gay members, expand their platform to take on human rights more broadly, and educate the public about equal protections for gays rather than foregrounding marriage as their major political goal. Groups also said they would take a cautious approach to sponsoring legal challenges at the state level, focusing on civil unions instead of marriage. At this juncture, activists said they were generally concerned that challenging and even winning these propositions in court would only fuel a conservative backlash, "like pouring gasoline onto the fire for purposes of the federal marriage amendment" (Liptak, 2004).

In the aftermath of the November 2004 election, conservatives continued to push state-by-state for amendments banning same-sex marriages. As a result, several other states like Indiana and Iowa that already had laws banning gay marriage also rapidly pushed to amend their state constitution to ensure that same-sex unions would not gain legal rights, benefits, or protections. During the midterm election in November 2006, several other states passed constitutional amendments banning same-sex marriages, including Colorado, Idaho, South Carolina, South Dakota, Tennessee, Virginia, and Wisconsin.

In 2008 media outlets around the country focused intently on the activity surrounding California's Proposition 8, the most expensive ballot proposition of the year. Prop 8 proponents sought to overturn the May 2008 California Supreme Court ruling that had legalized same-sex marriages in the state. On November 5, along with securing the election of President Barack Obama, 52 percent of the state's voters also voted "yes" to the constitutional amendment outlawing gay marriages. Hoping for similar results, same-sex-marriage opponents in Maine organized a referendum that in November 2009 brought the issue to public vote, which also narrowly passed and banned gay marriages in that state.

Despite these losses, gay rights proponents scored several legislative and judicial victories in 2008 and 2009. In this time period, garnering widespread news media attention, Connecticut, Iowa, Vermont, and New Hampshire legalized same-sex unions (Connecticut and Iowa as a result of state supreme court rulings; Vermont and New Hampshire through their state legislatures). Maine's state legislature also legalized gay marriages in May 2009, but the vote was overturned by the public referendum in November 2009.

In March 2010 Washington, D.C., joined these five states (Connecticut, Iowa, Massachusetts, New Hampshire, and Vermont) in granting marriage licenses to same-sex couples. In June 2011 New York became the sixth and largest state to legalize same-sex marriages after the state GOP–controlled senate voted in favor of a gay marriage bill. At the time of this writing, gay marriage in California has recently been restored, yet legal challenges remain. In August 2010, U.S. District Court Judge Vaughn Walker struck down the voter initiative as unconstitutional, but Prop 8 proponents appealed the decision. In December 2012, the U.S. Supreme Court agreed to hear the California case, as well as another case from New York state. These decisions, announced in June of 2013, solidified two major victories for the gay rights movement and have been hailed as landmark cases for civil rights. The Supreme Court struck down the Clinton-era Defense of Marriage Act (DOMA) as unconstitutional. In addition, arguing that Prop 8 sponsors did not have legal standing to defend the initiative in court, the justices dismissed the appeal and by extension resumed same-sex marriages in California.

The Supreme Court decisions followed the Obama administration's announcement two years prior that it would no longer defend the constitutionality of DOMA. In March 2011, in what U.S. news media dubbed a "policy reversal," Obama said the act violated the equal protection clause of the Fifth Amendment. This declaration came on the heels of the Congressional repeal of the "Don't Ask Don't Tell" policy, ending the 17-year law that banned gays and lesbians from serving openly in the military.

One year later the Obama administration's position on same-sex marriage was overtly clarified. In what the *New York Times* referred to as "a wrenching personal transformation on the issue," in May 2012 Obama told the American public that he supports gay marriage (Calmes & Baker, 2012). After two years of saying that his views were "evolving," Obama said his public proclamation was driven by conversations with his gay friends, his wife, and daughters. In a sit-down interview on ABC's *Good Morning America,* he told Robin Roberts, "At a certain point, I've just concluded that for me personally it is important for me to go ahead and affirm that I think same-sex couples should be able to get married" (Calmes & Baker, 2012).

Political strategists and reporters speculated that it was Vice President Joe Biden who forced the president's hand on the issue, as just 48 hours earlier Biden had broadcast his backing of gay marriage on the Sunday morning talk show *Meet the Press*. Obama's "transformation" on the issue was in many ways not all that surprising, considering his leadership in repealing the military's "Don't Ask, Don't Tell" policy and his reversal on DOMA. Many voters already presumed that the president supported marriage rights for same-sex couples and that his proclamation wasn't tied to specific policy initiatives. As Massachusetts senator Barney Frank said, "'Politically, it's kind of a nonevent'" (Calmes & Baker, 2012).

Yet the symbolic significance of the first sitting president—and the first African American president at that—to openly acknowledge his support for marriage equality was hard to dismiss. The president threw one of the most politically charged social issues into the ring yet again, during what was expected to be a close election, risking an unpredictable fallout (Calmes & Baker, 2012). However, as the results of the 2012 election indicated, the president's move wasn't that risky after all. Obama was reelected by a comfortable margin, and for the first time in history, three states approved gay marriage measures at the ballot box—Maryland, Maine, and Washington—bringing the total number to nine states where same-sex marriage is legal. Obama's second term began with his resolute support for same-sex marriage and gay rights more broadly, the first president to take up both in an inaugural address (see concluding chapter).

The battles that continue to wage surrounding these legal and political events have kept the issue of same-sex-marriage rights at the center of cultural debate and in the media spotlight. This evolving coverage of contemporary gay civil rights issues like military inclusion and gay marriage in the 2000s unfolded against a backdrop of increased gay-themed programming in mainstream entertainment media. In order to understand the battle over marriage in the news media, it is first important to consider the significance of this rise of gay images and narratives in the media.

The Rise of Gay-Themed Media

The debate over same-sex-marriage rights has erupted during a period of unprecedented visibility for gays and lesbians in the news and popular culture, what cultural studies scholars have dubbed "the era of the visible" (Becker, 2006; Gross, 2001; Walters, 2001a). From countless television hits like *Queer Eye for the Straight Guy, Modern Family,* and *The L Word,* to cable channels that promise "all gay, all the time" (LOGO), to popular "out" celebrities like Ellen DeGeneres, who graced the cover of *People* magazine with her bride, Portia DeRossi, America appears to be in the midst of a "gay moment" (Becker, 2006).

However, the rise in entertainment appeal and the recognition of gays and lesbians as a budding consumer market has not necessarily challenged homophobia or worked to combat heterosexual privilege. As a line of critical cultural work has argued (Alwood, 1996; Barnhurst, 2003; Becker, 2006; Gross, 2001; Sender, 2004; Walters, 2001a), gay and lesbian visibility in the media is paradoxical, simultaneously symbolizing "the sign of social decay and the chic flavor of the month" (Walters, 2001a, p. 14). Despite the great critical and commercial success of gay-themed programming like *Ellen* and *Will & Grace* in the 1990s, and *Queer as Folk* and *The L Word* in the 2000s, social and civil rights struggles for gay and lesbian citizens have continued. Anti-gay legislative measures, like the passage of the federal Defense of Marriage Act and the dozens of state bans on gay marriage, have proliferated. Hate crimes against the gay community continue to rise despite the explosion of gay images in entertainment media.

Building on this growing body of work (Aarons, 2003; Alwood, 1996; Becker, 2006; Bennet, 2000; Gross, 2001; Keller & Stratyner, 2006; Sender, 2004; Walters, 2001a, 2001b), my look at the gay marriage debate in the news is first and foremost dedicated to studying the politics of representation, which is concerned not only with *who gets seen* in the media and popular culture but also "what it *means* to be seen after all" (Ciasullo, 2001, p. 605). Work from feminist and queer theorists has shown us how the mass media and popular culture have historically served as powerful and instrumental sites for regulating the boundaries of gendered and sexual identities, what it means to be "male" or "female," "straight" or "gay." Since media representations are always a part of larger hegemonic power structures, marginal groups must conform to the rules of dominant culture to gain *visibility,* often mistaken as *acceptance.* Constructions of gendered, raced, classed, and sexual identities in the news and popular culture operate within an overall set of power relations that privilege reproduction and heterosexuality (Rubin, 1989). "To be sure, representation promises visibility, but visibility means not only that one is present but that one is being watched"; inevitably, "certain images get singled out as watchable" (Ciasullo, 2001).

As this line of work reveals, images of the lesbian, gay, bisexual and transgender (LGBT) community in the media, consistent with other marginalized groups, were virtually nonexistent a mere half century ago. Gay issues, now routinely front-page news, were considered "unfit to print" 60 years ago by

America's widely read newspapers and magazines. When representations did begin to emerge, they perpetuated a host of anti-gay stereotypes. In *Straight News* Edward Alwood (1996) shows how, much like early film and television, gays and lesbians emerged in the news as objects of derision and scorn: sexual perverts on par with child molesters and rapists, mentally deranged criminals, immoral sinners, and as a threat to the social order. Gays have also been routinely constructed as victims of abuse and disease—first as sufferers of mental illness in the 1950s and eventually as victims of the human immunodeficiency virus/acquired immunodeficiency syndrome (HIV/AIDS) in the 1980s—trapped against their will in a dangerous and corrupt lifestyle. From underreporting the numbers at gay rights marches by relying on "official" police estimates rather than those of organizers, to trivializing the 1969 Stonewall riots, scholars have suggested that mainstream news organizations have historically participated in disparaging and marginalizing gay activist efforts (Alwood, 1996; Gross & Woods, 1999). Reporting on gay and lesbian issues has inevitably been colored by what Alwood (1996) calls a "heterosexual assumption," since newsrooms have historically been run by white, middle-class, heterosexual men.

Beginning in the 1940s, when homosexuality emerged as a topic of media reports, gay identity was characterized as a threat to national security and as a mental disorder. News stories centered on army regulations to forbid gay recruits from serving during World War II (Bennet, 2000). In another widely cited example, in the 1950s "homosexuality became synonymous with communism" during McCarthy-era concerns over communists and "perverts" infiltrating top government agencies (Gross & Woods, 1999, citing a report in the *New York Times,* April 19, 1950). One of the first television appearances by gay men was the 1967 hour-long documentary "The Homosexual" hosted by CBS's Mike Wallace. Famously, while the program excluded lesbians altogether, the gay men who did appear were hidden behind strategically placed potted plants, their voices disguised as they confessed their "sickness" to television audiences (Gross & Woods, 1999, p. 350). In 1969 the riots protesting the police raid of the Stonewall Inn were hard to ignore, as many attribute these events to igniting the gay liberation movement. Yet the *New York Times* buried coverage of the riots in a brief article on page 33, while the *New York Post* sensationalized the protests with the headline "Homo Nest Raided! Queen Bees Stinging Mad" (Alwood, 1996).

This sort of underreporting and misrepresentation was tied largely to the fact that LGBT journalists remained closeted in the newsroom, fearful of the repercussions of coming out in a discriminatory workplace environment (Alwood, 1996; Leibler et al., 2009). The widespread devastation of the AIDS epidemic in the 1980s, however, forced many LGBT reporters out of the closet. The AIDS crisis was initially ignored by the mainstream press when the disease was thought to be contained to marginalized subcultures. Eventually coverage routinely characterized the gay population as "walking time bombs," an at-risk group that threatened to spread their plague to the rest of society's "innocent victims" (Edward Albert, as cited in Gross & Woods, 1999, p. 397).

Over the past two decades, gay and lesbian citizens and spokespersons have appeared openly on the news with regularity. However, some activists argue that contemporary journalistic filming of the community, which shoots subjects from the back, hiding their faces from view, imbues homosexuality with an element of shame (see discussion in chapter 2). Even in the 1990s, when news stories began to focus more on public policy and civil rights issues like serving in the military, job discrimination, and hate crimes legislation, tired stereotypical images and exoticized representations lingered in the media. "For too many years when gay men and lesbians appeared on the nightly news, their lives were illustrated by woefully archaic film clips of seedy gay bars or seminaked parade revelers. Even through the late 1990s it used to amaze me that journalists could yammer about employment legislation or 'don't ask, don't tell' while showing film clips of drag queens in hot pink beehive hairdos and spiked heels" (Jacobs, 2004, p. 72).

Increased media attention on gay civil rights struggles has been a prominent component of this contemporary era of visibility. In the past decade, several book-length volumes have interrogated the cultural, political, and economic impulses of the 1990s and 2000s that produced this rise in gay-themed programming (Becker, 2006; Gross, 2001; Walters, 2001a). As Suzanna Walters argues in *All the Rage* (2001a), gay and lesbian identity has moved from invisibility to that of public spectacle. Although shows like *Ellen* and *Will & Grace* offered more varied representations than in the past, these depictions were constructed to make homosexuality more palatable to a straight audience rather than questioning the values of a heteronormative society (Battles & Hilton-Murrow, 2002; Dow, 2001). As with other marginalized groups, these programs situated gayness within the "safe and familiar popular culture conventions" of the situation comedy (Battles & Hilton-Murrow, 2002, p. 87). In other words, gay and lesbian identity has been written into a straight world, with representations largely crafted to appeal to a heterosexual culture (Clark, 1995; Kates, 1999).

Moreover, consumerist media representations have perpetuated an image of the LGBT community within a narrow range of discourses about gender, race, class, and sexuality. As Larry Gross (2001) argues, "Gay people did not . . . ascend from the pariah status of criminal, sinner, and pervert to the respectable categories of voting bloc and market niche without playing the familiar American game of assimilation" (p. xvi). To be gay in the media has meant you are young, white, and wealthy, oftentimes male, severed from the larger LGBT community, and removed from queer politics.

For example, in the late 1990s the popular ABC sitcom *Ellen* (1994–1998) featured the first leading lesbian character on mainstream television. Critics celebrated Ellen DeGeneres's coming out, both as herself and as Ellen Morgan, her character on the show, as a watershed moment for gay and lesbian representation. As Dow (2001) argues, however, DeGeneres's coming out was anchored to heteronormative power relationships that demanded imposed conformity to her straight viewing audience. The character Ellen Morgan's coming out had to abide by certain rules of gay and lesbian representation, rules that make homosexuality less threatening to dominant culture: she was largely desexualized, as physical contact with another woman was rarely shown, and she was apolitical, as her coming out was personal and divorced from any sort of LGBT political movement. Ellen Morgan comes out in a straight world, isolated from a larger LGBT community. Her gay "confession" was presented as a "problem" for straight culture, her family, and friends. Much like *The Cosby Show* was written for the comfort of white audiences, *Ellen* was crafted to appeal to straight audiences (Dow 2001). Nevertheless, ABC pulled the show from the air in 1998, citing declining ratings and increased pressure from conservative groups about the program's gay content.

Likewise, *Will & Grace* (1998–2006), NBC's popular sitcom about the relationship between a gay male lawyer and his best friend, a hetero female interior designer, was lauded as boundary-breaking. The series contained not one, but two gay male leads, who performed markedly different gay personas—Will was presented as more masculine, serious, and "straight," while Jack was presented as stereotypically feminine, flighty, and catty. However, as Kathleen Battles and Wendy Hilton-Murrow (2002) point out, this "gay" show operated within heteronormative power structures. The relationships were organized along heterosocial pairings; the male/female couplings of Will and Grace, and of Jack and Karen, were key to the show's logics. Like *Ellen,* the show foregrounded interpersonal relationships over larger political aims. Will's coming out was presented almost exclusively as a problem for Grace, devoid of a critique of the larger systemic homophobia at work.

This scholarship points to the potentially dangerous downside of increased media attention: that visibility comes at a price, and that it is often sorely mistaken for cultural acceptance and inclusive citizenship (Clark, 1995; Dow, 2001; Fejes, 2000; Gross, 2001; Walters, 2001a, 2001b). Media narratives celebrate a post–gay rights era, assuming that civil rights struggles have been won and equality has been achieved. What results is a culture eager to consume "the *images* of gay life but all too reluctant to embrace the *realities* of gay identities" (Walters, 2001a, p. 10; emphasis in original).

In the 2000s we have seen the development of what one volume dubbed "the new queer aesthetic on television" (Keller & Stratyner, 2006), the television and marketing industries' embrace of sexually provocative, hip, and "edgy" programming designed to appeal to younger, cosmopolitan audiences. Shows like *Queer as Folk* and *The L Word* play by different rules than those of the more "sanitized" world of network television, produced for premium cable audiences with more adventurous and sexually explicit themes. Marketers are using the allure of gay culture to appeal to trendy, neoliberal straight audiences just as "companies like Nike and Sprite have used elements of hip-hop culture to entice white audiences" (Robert Benjamin Bateman, in Keller and Stratyner, 2006, p. 14; see also Clark, 1995; Kates, 1999). As Ron Becker (2010) writes, "Television's seemingly ubiquitous openly gay men and the gay friendly straight people who surround them reconfirm a liberal notion that the closet is gone and the homophobia that constructed it is increasingly irrelevant" (p. 13).

Scholars who have turned to more recent coverage of gay issues have found that media tend to present LGBT communities and issues in ways that "don't challenge hegemonic notions of gender and sexuality, and by employing frames that privilege heterosexuality" (Leibler et al., 2009, p. 256; see also Barnhurst, 2003; Schwartz, 2011). For example, Barnhurst's (2003) study of National Public Radio reporting on LGBT issues across three election cycles found that the sheer number of stories and the length of stories increased from 1992 to 2000. However, this coverage was a "mixed blessing": the professionalization of LGBT sources normalized gay perspectives but also made resistance to dominant heterosexist institutions unlikely. The polarization of gay issues in news reports also resulted in the ratcheting up of hateful and homophobic rhetoric by anti-gay sources. Likewise, Liebler and his colleagues' (2009) analysis of the same-sex-marriage debate in 2004 found that daily newspapers and wire stories tended to depoliticize the issue. News stories employed assimilationist and normalizing narratives that insisted that LGBT citizens are "just like everybody else." Nonconfrontational sources privileged "hegemonic ways of seeing," failing to mount a critique of the exclusive and heteronormative nature of marriage (p. 670).

Considering the history of media representations and the coverage of gay issues in the press, the debate over marriage offers the opportunity to once again become front-page news and to advance the conversation over gay rights in public discourse. As one young gay activist wrote in an editorial for *Newsweek* during the 2004 election, "That's why many are happy about the gay marriage debate: it's a good way for the gay community to rally for its cause and raise its public profile. Previously beneath the radar screen, the prominence attached to gay issues in the [2004] presidential campaign is putting . . . the community at the center of the political debate" (Mosvick, 2004).

As history suggests, and as that activist argues, media representations and news coverage in particular are critical components in becoming a player in the cultural scene. The unprecedented amount of reporting on the issue of same-sex marriage creates a space in political culture for gays and lesbians to make headlines in ways they never have before: not as "criminals" perverting children, not as "victims" of a deadly disease, not as exoticized drag queens parading proudly, but potentially as fully human couples engaged in loving relationships and raising families.

However, following the work of critical cultural scholars, I investigate how the marriage conversation has not only provided new opportunities but has also constrained discourses surrounding gay and lesbian identity. As the gay rights movement has moved away from a separatist stance critical of dominant culture, organizations have more recently focused on moderate political strategies that highlight similarities to the straight majority (see discussion in chapter 2, as well as Armstrong, 2002; Bernstein, 1997). Media strategies within the movement now center on mainstreaming and normalizing gay and lesbian identity, forging alliances with non-gay organizations, and educating the public about issues that are important to the LGBT community. By exploring the aims, strategies, and stories of gay rights activists, I join a larger conversation about the consequences of social movements' reliance on the commercial news media to enter the political debate and shape public discourse.

Media Frames and Social Movements

This book is also informed by a theoretical interest in media framing, or the process of organizing and assigning meaning to issues and events (see, for example, Entman, 1992; Entman & Rojecki, 1993; W. Gamson, 1998; Goffman, 1974; Graber, 1997; Iyengar, 1991; Snow & Benford, 1988; Tuchman, 1976; Weaver, 2007). Communication scholars have long recognized that newsmakers do more than *report* events. News functions as a narrative, literary form that provides symbolic definitions of social realities. Like other cultural storytellers, journalists rely on standard, familiar stories and symbolic representations that media audiences use to make sense of events and issues. Newsmakers are governed by news values that dictate that the most extraordinary, dramatic, and tragic elements of stories will be emphasized. For these unusual and otherwise meaningless occurrences to make sense, they must be given order and meaning; otherwise, they remain random, isolated events.

Those who study the media and social movements have paid special attention to how journalists frame social issues, movement goals, and activist participants (see, for example, Bronstein, 2005; W. Gamson, 1998; Mansbridge 1986; McLeod, 1995; Snow & Benford, 1988; Sobieraj, 2011). Researchers have found that the framing of social issues by newsmakers "shapes public understanding of the roots of contemporary problems and the merits of alternative solutions" (Nelson & Kinder, 1996, p. 1055). Coverage of a movement or issue can have an impact on public support for the cause, influence policy makers to act, and affect the group's ability to attract and retain members. For example, writing about the American women's movement, Carolyn Bronstein (2005) shows how news frames radicalized movement members, cast protesters as social deviants, and ultimately weakened public support for feminism. As she points out, framing does not remain static, but rather evolves as "journalists often restructure frames to match changing social and political conditions" (p. 785), especially for ongoing social issues. Most recently, Sarah Sobieraj's *Soundbitten: The Perils of Media-Centered Political Activism* (2011) tracked fifty activist organizations across two campaign cycles, critiquing groups' aggressive and often ineffective pursuit of media publicity.

Extending this body of work on media framing and social movements, this project is concerned with how the gay marriage debate has been organized and given meaning by media storytellers. In the 2000s the marriage equality movement, and the broader gay rights movement as well, experienced "its definitional moment" in the mainstream press, "during which journalists explain and appraise it" (Bronstein, 2005, p. 785). Based on in-depth interviews with the leading gay rights activists who were on the "front lines" of the marriage debate, this study documents the inner workings of the marriage equality movement to reveal the internal debates that social movements inevitably face when they find themselves in the glare of mainstream media: What stories do we tell about our lives? What images best represent our community? Who should speak for us? This study thus offers a significant contribution to the study of media and social activism. I show how activist frames, messages, and tactics evolve over time in response to the gay marriage controversy and its onslaught of media attention.

Marriage in the Mainstream

Marriage is an institution that has historically served as a civil rights battlefield. As conservative columnist and gay rights spokesperson Andrew Sullivan (2004) points out, African Americans were able to gain access to marriage only after the desegregation of other core public institutions like the military and the education system. "The fact that the constitutionality of interracial marriage was *the last* of these cultural milestones to be established is therefore far from remarkable. The symbolic power of marriage, it turns out, is even deeper than that of citizenship, even starker than that of military glory, even clearer than that of public space. It is the institution where public citizenship most dramatically intersects with private self-definition. It is where people have historically drawn the line" (p. xxv).

The battle over gay marriage therefore sheds light on national discourses concerning the institution of marriage itself at a time when traditional heterosexual hierarchies are being simultaneously bolstered and disputed. As Barry Adam (2003) writes, "Marriage has long been implicated in a politics of exclusion. Nation-building rhetoric employing analogies of the nation to the family (and thus marriage) inevitably manufactures a series of 'others' thrown out of the national family and uses marriage laws as a tool to mark that exclusion" (p. 274).

As historians and sociologists remind us (Coontz, 2005; Weiss, 2000), marriage has always signified much more than apolitical love and intimacy; it has historically served as the central mechanism in the organization of social and economic life. Gay nuptials are only the latest in a long litany of complaints bemoaning the "besieged" institution of marriage. For many social conservatives, gay marriage represents the final "nail in the coffin" of marriage and the family, joining other discourses of social crises such as high divorce rates, premarital sexual relations, children born out of wedlock, and working mothers.

This conversation about gay marriage thus invariably reflects our culture's growing ambivalence about the institution of marriage itself and its place in our modern society. At a time when any marriage in the United States is statistically more likely to fail than succeed, the number of unmarried people is greater than the number of married people, and celebrities popularize rush-to-the-altar weekend weddings that end in divorce by midweek, the debate over same-sex nuptials in the 2000s is intertwined with, not separate from, this overall cultural hand-wringing over marriage.

As Ron Becker (2006) aptly points out, "gay TV" (the recent rise of gay-themed television programming) reveals as much about straight America as it does about the gay and lesbian characters featured in it. These civil rights battles—over gays and lesbians in the military, over equal employment, over marriage rights—reflect and contribute to America's "straight panic," what Becker defines as the growing anxieties felt by a heterosexual culture that is "confronting this shifting social landscape where categories of sexual identity were repeatedly scrutinized and traditional moral hierarchies regulating sexuality were challenged" (p. 4). As I revisit in the concluding chapter, our culture's gay marriage debates that are carried out in the media both reflect and contribute to an overall uneasiness about the institution of marriage itself losing the "exceptional" status it has long enjoyed.

It is within the context of these larger bodies of work—the rise of LGBT visibility in the media, the shifting goals and strategies of the gay rights movement, the role of marriage as a political and social institution, and the media framing of issues and movements—that this book investigates media coverage of the gay marriage issue and activist discourses surrounding it. I examine these news narratives as a gateway into contemporary understandings of gay and lesbian identity—namely, who is allowed in and who is cast out of our "national family."

Research Approach

Inspired in part by Todd Gitlin's (1980) canonical work on the complex relations between the news media and social movements, this book is interested in how the major news media covered the controversial issue of same-sex marriage and how activist message-producers struggled to promote their preferred meanings, definitions, and images in news discourse. My work is not designed to determine a cause-and-effect relationship between the news media and the gay rights movement. Rather, I approach these entities, as Gitlin says, not as "determined objects 'having impacts' on each other, as if movements and media were billiard balls, but [as] an active movement and active media pressing on each other, sometimes deliberately, sometimes not, in a process rich with contradiction and self-contradiction" (p. 14).

In order to explore how marginalized groups work with media to shape news coverage of their cause and their community, I started by conducting in-depth, face-to-face interviews with gay rights activists who had become media spokespersons for the marriage equality issue. As I detail in chapter 2, I spoke with those activists who had been granted a voice in the mainstream news debate, those whom prominent news entities had hand-selected to represent "the gay voice" in what was constructed as a two-sided conflict. These were the groups and the spokespersons who were "on the Rolodex," so to speak, of major national news organizations. I wanted to interview the "elite" of the gay establishment—those individuals who were in a position to sell their issue, their story, and their version of gay and lesbian identity to the American public. I spoke with the presidents, communications directors, press secretaries, national news directors, religion and faith directors, media relations directors, and board members of the nation's leading LGBT organizations.

I traveled to New York, Boston, Washington, D.C., and San Francisco in 2005 to interview these activists, shortly after the events of 2004 that pushed the issue into the mainstream media. Based upon the shifting legal and cultural climate in 2008 and 2009, I returned to interview those same informants in 2010 to examine how the aims and challenges of gay rights activists had shifted during this time frame—their goals, the stories they attempted to communicate about gay and lesbian life, and their analysis of media coverage of LGBT issues and communities. I also added to my list of informants several new voices that had emerged in this debate over those five years. In total, I conducted 30 interviews with representatives from organizations like Lambda Legal; Freedom to Marry; the Gay and Lesbian Alliance Against Defamation (GLAAD); Marriage Equality New York; the Task Force; Human Rights Campaign; Victory Fund; Gay and Lesbian Activists Alliance (GLAA); Parents, Families and Friends of Lesbians and Gays (PFLAG); and the Log Cabin Republicans (see the appendix for a list of organizations and informants interviewed). Through in-depth interviews, I investigated questions such as:

- How did gay and lesbian rights activists decide to foreground one goal in the media—same-sex marriage—over other goals of the movement (e.g., employment nondiscrimination, HIV/AIDS research funding, equal housing, and the like)?
- What were the predominant stories activists tried to tell about gay and lesbian life? In doing so, what challenges did they face from reporters, from their political opponents, and from critics within their own community?
- How did activists select the couples and the images that came to represent the marriage equality movement? How did they try to symbolize same-sex ceremonies in the news?
- In the views of activists, what strategies and stories were successful in garnering media attention and appealing to a mainstream audience, and which ones ultimately failed?
- How did activists characterize coverage of the debate? What aspects of media coverage were they happy with, and what disappointed them?

Next, to investigate news content, I relied primarily on textual analysis to critique the symbolic meanings of narratives and images that were used to tell the story of same-sex marriage in news features. As I detail in chapters 3, 4, and 5, I examined hundreds of stories from national newsmagazines like *Time, Newsweek,* and *U.S. News & World Report*; front-page stories from leading national newspapers like the *New York Times, Washington Post,* and *USA Today*; episodes of prime-time television news programs like *60 Minutes* and *Nightline*; and segments of national network television news. I selected programs and publications that were prominent, had high impact, and appealed to a large national news audience. I analyzed news texts from two different time periods across the decade (2003–2004 and again in 2008–2010) to capture the major legal and political developments in the United States that made the same-sex-marriage issue a front-page story. Specifically, I investigated the following:

- Who were the prominent figures and groups allowed to participate in the national media debate? Whose voices were privileged in news discourses about gay marriage?
- What were the dominant framing devices used to structure the debate for news audiences?
- How were labels, images, and descriptive language used in news stories to portray the LGBT community?
- What were the physical and demographic characteristics of the gay and lesbian couples selected to represent the marriage movement?
- What kinds of visual images of gay and lesbian life did the news media foreground?
- How were standard visual symbols (rings, cakes, flowers) and dress (wedding gowns and tuxedos) used to represent same-sex ceremonies in the news?

Like all research projects, this project has its limitations. My approach is in some ways too narrow and in other ways overly broad. Focusing my interviews on prominent gay rights activists who already had a voice in the mainstream media clearly excluded many other kinds of groups and activists. For example, I did not interview gay marriage opponent groups like Focus on the Family and the National Organization for Marriage. I also did not interview those lesbian, gay, bisexual, transgender, and queer (LGBTQ) organizations largely silenced in the mainstream debate over marriage, those groups whose members were either opposed to state-sanctioned marriage or believe the movement should focus on other priorities. Also omitted are the journalists, editors, reporters, news photographers, and videographers who covered the gay marriage issue. Each of these groups has the potential to offer important perspectives on representations of gay marriage in the media and provide a promising program for future research.

In addition, my approach to studying the issue of gay marriage in the *news* is but one way to examine the larger public debate about the issue. News narratives are only one important aspect of the overall ideological landscape. Other narratives surrounding gay marriage emerged in popular culture during this time, including those in entertainment television, feature film, documentary film, on websites, and in discourses over legal court cases (see, for example, Bennett, 2006; and Walters, 2001a, 2001b).

Also, by focusing on *mainstream* news discourses—those programs and publications that reach the largest news audiences—I eliminated coverage of the gay marriage issue in smaller, more progressive news outlets that may have included diverse perspectives and a larger universe of frames. I did not focus on how the issue was covered by alternative media written for and targeted to the LGBTQ community, publications such as *Out* or the *Advocate*.

Just as no analysis can claim to be representative of "the media" (all media coverage of an issue, for example), no study of media *content* can capture the various ways audiences construct meanings of those messages, images, and stories. My approach strove to unpack the dominant meanings about the gay marriage issue that were embedded in mainstream news narratives during this volatile time period. My analysis here, then, represents only one piece, but a significant piece, in the puzzle of how social movement actors define a controversial issue in cultural politics and attempt to shape public discourse through the mainstream news media.

Plan of the Book

This book about media coverage of the gay marriage issue begins with the story of how activists came to define marriage equality as a central goal of the movement in the first place. Chapter 2 reveals how most activists were initially reluctant to "do battle" over marriage in what they termed the "oppositional environment" of the mainstream press, an issue forced into the media spotlight by opponent groups and sensationalistic media outlets. However, activists eventually saw the marriage issue as a potential corrective to the salacious images of gay and lesbian life they had seen perpetuated in the press and popular culture. Attempts to craft "positive" narratives and images about couples and families brought about intra-community struggles over how to best define gay relationships, how to talk about marriage, and which stories would resonate with mainstream news audiences.

How successful activists were in framing the debate and producing their preferred images for the news media are the subjects of chapters 3 and 4. In chapter 3 I examine the face of gay marriage that emerged in news texts, how gay and lesbian couples, families, and communities were visually represented in news stories. In particular I examine how markers of gender, class, race, lifestyle, and sexuality were deployed to present particular gay and lesbian couples as "deserving" of marriage. While these "poster couples" selected by news producers and gay rights activists were oftentimes legitimated in news narratives, they were also cast as "different" from the more "radical" community of non-married gays, relegating particular LGBT and queer identities to the margins.

Despite these attempts to "mainstream" gay marriage, chapter 4 shows how activists fell prey to the common pitfalls that have historically plagued reporting of social movements. Media analysis shows how standard journalistic frames highlighted a simplistic, two-sided conflict that silenced alternative perspectives; provided a platform for recycled homophobic rhetoric; and framed the issue within "official" institutions of power that have historically criminalized and marginalized the gay community. Journalistic definitions of authority, expertise, and "balance" created an uneven playing field, pitting gay and lesbian spokespersons against unequal sources of influence from legal, medical, religious, and political authorities.

As activists recognized, doing battle over marriage in the mainstream media meant conforming to the rules of news making. This ultimately led to tensions over representations and media strategies, especially in the wake of losing Proposition 8 in California in 2008 and Question 1 in Maine the following year. In chapter 5 I return in 2010 to interview those activist informants, as well as talk with new activist voices that emerged in this debate, in order to reveal how media narratives and activist strategies evolved over time. While the issue no longer had the same kind of novel, sensationalistic "freak show" coverage that prevailed early on in the debate, problematic framing devices of "God vs. gays" and "blacks vs. gays" dominated coverage. Movement leaders faced internal conflicts over how best to represent pro-gay perspectives in media discourse and gain support from the "moveable middle."

Over a decade ago, social critic Michael Warner (1999) argued in *The Trouble with Normal: Sex, Politics, and the Ethics of Queer Life* that gay marriage would ultimately work to create hierarchies between the "good gays," who settle down, get married, and rear children, and the "bad gays," who continue to live out their "alternative" lifestyles on the margins of society. In chapter 6 I conclude the book by questioning the limits of commercial media as a route to social change, and by critiquing the institution of marriage as a route to inclusive citizenship. I argue that these images and narratives employed in both activist strategies and news discourses may unwittingly work to stigmatize those (unmarried) lesbian, gay, bisexual, transgender, and queer citizens who do not fit the normative mold in this new era of visibility.

2. Fighting the "Battle to Be Boring"

Marriage as a Portal into the Mainstream

The scariest thing is when you start reading in the paper how
normal you are, and you start to believe it.

—Arlene, Massachusetts Gay and Lesbian Political Caucus

In the office suite of the gay and lesbian rights organization Freedom to
Marry, I waited patiently for my first interview to begin. Across the table from
me sat Samiya, the organization's young communications director, who was
rifling through the paperwork I had sent her before the interview. Her brow
furrowed, she picked up her pen and began to circle and cross out several
words. She made some notations in the margins, then signed her name on
the line to indicate that she agreed to participate in the study. As she handed
the papers back to me, I noticed she had circled words like "challenge" (as in
challenge a dominant institution) and "redefine" (as in redefine marriage)
in the project description and had drawn frowny faces in the margins to
mark her disapproval of my semantic inaccuracies. She pointedly explained,
"We're not defining or redefining the institution of marriage . . . marriage
is a living, breathing institution, and it's been changing ever since it started
up through now . . . And I think it's absolutely kind of a right-wing point
of our opposition to act like we're redefining marriage when we don't have
that power . . . I think World War II changed marriage more than we ever
will. Women's equality movement changed marriage at least as much, if not
more than, we ever will."

In this chapter I explore how leading gay and lesbian social movement
leaders staged the issue of gay marriage—how they crafted narratives about
same-sex marriage, and about gay and lesbian life, for mainstream media
audiences. This chapter also communicates a story of struggle—not only

the battles that activists waged with their political opponents over marriage rights; not only the challenges they faced in trying to tell their stories in a heterosexist commercial media system; but also about the internal debates, the kind that are hidden from the glare of media coverage, about how to define, construct, and symbolize same-sex marriages. Because of the centrality of the news media in producing and propelling the same-sex-marriage debate into the public consciousness, I examine news content not only as the major source of this investigation but also as "a constitutive medium of the debate itself and of the imaginary within which it took form" (Strassler, 2004, p. 691).

As I detail later in this chapter, the LGBT movement, like other minority and civil rights movements, has depended in part upon recognition in the media to become players in democratic politics and public culture. When groups do emerge from the shadows of invisibility, "the manner of their representation will reflect the biases and interests of those powerful people who define the public agenda," mostly white, middle-age, heterosexual males who hold middle- to upper-class positions in society (Gross, 2001, p. 4). How social activists navigate this uneven terrain is a central concern of this book.

In this chapter I analyze in-depth interviews that took place with social movement actors in 2005. My respondents were involved in shaping the same-sex-marriage debate in national news stories at a crucial time when the issue first exploded in media discourse and political debate, in 2003 and 2004. Later in the book, in chapter 5, I report the findings from interviews with these same activists and with several new voices that emerged in 2009 and 2010 in order to interrogate how activist strategies and discourses evolved over this time frame.

I selected my informants by first analyzing broadcast news stories about the gay marriage issue in order to determine those activists who were cited as spokespersons for the LGBT community. For my initial round of interviews that took place in 2005, I examined more than 100 transcripts of *NBC*, *ABC*, and *CBS* nightly news broadcasts from 2003 and 2004, those stories included in my media content analysis (see chapter 3). I compiled a list of spokespersons who were housed within or attributed to gay rights organizations. Following Myra Marx Ferree and her colleagues' (2002) definition of standing, these were spokespersons who were directly quoted, appeared on camera, and were able to offer their own interpretations and definitions of events rather than simply being covered as an object of news investigation.

Initially I identified a total of 17 activists, representing 13 national gay rights organizations, who were cited, a number that struck me as smaller than I originally anticipated, considering the sheer number of news stories. The pool of "credible" gay rights spokespersons, as defined by mainstream news organizations, was relatively small, with the same names appearing time and again. Of these 17 cited, I was able to interview 11 informants, representing 6 major organizations, who were active in the marriage movement on a national level at that time—representatives from the Human Rights Campaign, the Task Force, the Massachusetts Gay and Lesbian Political Caucus, Gay and Lesbian Advocates and Defenders (GLAD), Freedom to Marry, and the Log Cabin Republicans (see the appendix for a more detailed description of the interview process). From October 2005 through January 2006, I traveled to Boston, New York, Washington, D.C., and Oakland, California, to interview activists in person.

For comparative purposes, I also interviewed one activist during this time frame who was based in Indianapolis, Indiana, near where I was living at the time. While all my other informants were located in large, urban, politically progressive cities of the East and West Coasts, I included this Indianapolis activist in my study in order to learn about the impact of the national media attention on a local gay rights organization in a politically conservative "red state."

My interviewees worked often and intimately with news media personnel; they were public relations directors, communication strategists, and the presidents or founders of leading gay rights organizations. These social actors were in many ways the media elite of the gay rights movement and the public face of the LGBT community—those who had a voice in the mainstream media and were responsible for shaping news coverage of the marriage issue. My respondents had a variety of media responsibilities, including pitching news stories, writing and disseminating press releases, providing sources, shooting and distributing video footage ("b-roll") of their community, conducting and publishing research on same-sex marriage, and developing media communication messages and strategies. They also organized press conferences, held media training sessions, staged rallies and protests for press attention, helped design same-sex ceremonies as media events, and "prepped" couples for media appearances.

All of these informants had appeared in at least one (but more often multiple) national network news appearances in 2003 and 2004. Because this time period represents when the gay marriage controversy really began to capture the public imagination, the following questions drove my analysis: How did these activists decide to foreground one goal—same-sex marriage—over others? For those within the movement who had the power to shape the commercial spaces that gays and lesbians inhabit, what were the predominant stories they tried to tell about gay and lesbian life? How did fighting the marriage battle in the arena of the mainstream news media reshape the aims and priorities of the organization? Addressing these questions, this chapter

contributes to a rich body of scholarship that explores why social movements come to rely on the news media to enter mainstream public debate,
the strategies they use, and the consequences they face in doing so.

As this chapter demonstrates, activists were overwhelmingly concerned
with how the increased media attention brought about by the controversial
issue of same-sex marriage would define and shape the LGBT community.
Arlene of the Massachusetts Gay and Lesbian Political Caucus, a regional
group out of Boston that lobbies state legislators on behalf of gay and lesbian
issues, described the tension in the movement over pursuing media strategies.
"I was always very insistent that we should never seek media for the sake of
media. You seek it for a purpose. Which is a controversial subject within our
community because there are some people who believe that media is good
no matter what. 'As long as we're there telling our story, it's a good thing.'
Well, it might or might not be. Is it reminding them of something we want
them to forget?"

As evident in Arlene's comment, the movement remained cautious about
stepping into the spotlight—concerned about the messages media producers
might send about the community, guarded against what kinds of negative
stereotypes might be reproduced. As subsequent interviews with gay and
lesbian rights leaders on the front lines of the marriage battle demonstrate,
the media attention surrounding the marriage issue shone the spotlight on
the LGBT community in such a way that it became impossible for activists
to avoid interactions with a heterosexist mass media system.

Long before the news media began buzzing over same-sex marriage, the
issue itself, far from being a united and undisputed goal of the gay rights
movement, was the center of an intra-community debate. In this chapter I
first focus on how these social actors came to settle on the marriage equality
issue, and how informants defined marriage not as a battle of choice but as
one they were forced to contend with. I show how activists fought to "mainstream" gay marriage within the confines of a heteronormative news system,
and how these tensions led to competing definitional strategies for talking
about marriage in the press. To begin I contextualize these contemporary
debates over messaging by discussing how the gay movement has historically
struggled about when—and how—to seek media publicity.

The U.S. Gay Movement and the Media in Perspective

In 2003 and 2004, when the battle over same-sex-marriage rights was heating
up, the majority of the nation's gay and lesbian rights groups were already
employing moderate, assimilationist, equal-rights strategies for earning a spot

on the playing fields of media, culture, and politics. As Larry Gross summarized in 2001, the "organized sector of lesbian and gay America has embraced assimilation as the realization of their ultimate goal" (p. xvi). At that time the large and powerful gay organizations were headed by a partnered professional woman with children, thus "presenting the face of middle-class normality and respectability" (p. xvi).

Of course, the gay rights movement has not always relied upon assimilationist strategies and goals. Social movements in the United States have historically fluctuated between competing political logics (Armstrong, 2002; Bernstein, 1997; W. Gamson, 1998), what Mary Bernstein (1997) refers to as wrestling between the compulsion to celebrate difference, often in opposition to mainstream culture, and the impulse to suppress those differences in order to assimilate. Rather than simply following one route or the other, movements often oscillate between these political pathways, or even pursue both simultaneously.

As the gay and lesbian movement in the United States has experienced these tensions, their goals and strategies for achieving social reform have changed accordingly. The post-Stonewall early liberation model, in which LGBT groups critiqued social norms and institutions, has eventually been replaced by an interest-group model that seeks equal rights (Armstrong, 2002; Bernstein, 1997; W. Gamson, 1998). Armstrong (2002) traces how the gay liberation movement (1969–1970) that grew out of the New Left followed a redistributive politics that relied on a critique of capitalism and took the position that "sexual liberation was only a part of a larger movement seeking economic, racial, and gender justice" (p. 57). This arm of the gay movement was utterly at odds with the single-issue, rights-oriented politics of the homophile movement in the late 1960s. Gay rights groups began to model themselves after interest group logics and worked within existing political institutions to extend rights to the LGBT community, as opposed to critiquing mainstream institutions as "futile and contaminating" (Armstrong, 2002, p. 77). The movement that once largely stood for cultural transformation through sexual revolution is now one that seeks to achieve political rights through single-issue, interest group strategies. As Bernstein (1997) argues, "The lesbian and gay movement seems largely to have abandoned its emphasis on difference from the straight majority in favor of a moderate politics that highlights similarities" (p. 531).

These competing impulses continue to shape the movement today (Epstein, 1996; W. Gamson, 1998). On the one hand, the predominant *ethnic/essentialist logic* of the gay and lesbian movement argues that identity is a fixed, natural essence and depends upon collective action for political gain. In this model

LGBT communities take on the form of a "quasi-ethnicity" with their own neighborhoods, parades, and festivals. On the other hand, this essentialist logic is opposed to "queer activism" that seeks to break apart identity categories and blur group boundaries. Under this *deconstructionist political logic* one can be liberated only by resisting the "minority" label (W. Gamson, 1998). Scholars have argued that rather than hindering the movement, the existence of both logics has been key to its survival, one that celebrates both diversity and unity (Armstrong, 2002; Bernstein, 1997; W. Gamson 1998). Paradoxically, in the game of identity politics, social categorization is both the means of empowerment and the source of oppression (W. Gamson, 1998).

These political logics play an important role in whether or not social movements seek media attention, their strategies for doing so, and how successful they are in achieving a voice in public discourse. Social movements are often plagued by what William Carroll and Robert Ratner (1999) refer to as an "asymmetrical dependency" on the mass media (p. 26). As Todd Gitlin (1980) argues in *The Whole World Is Watching*, beginning in the twentieth century, social movement actors came to realize their "need" for mainstream mass communications in order to matter. Often groups attempting to reform society rely on media publicity to attract and mobilize group members, bring their issue(s) into the realm of public debate, assert their voice in a preexisting debate, educate the public about their cause, and influence policy decision makers. This dependency on the media may be even more extreme for groups who lack direct access to traditional political structures (such as the courts and the legislature), often the case with movements that define themselves in opposition to social institutions. For these actors who don't have a seat at the political table, the media may be the only route—albeit an indirect one—to social change.

The gay and lesbian movement in the United States has relied upon media attention in varying ways throughout its development. As with other movements, the media contributed to the gay movement in its infancy by helping to create its collective identity—by attracting, organizing, and mobilizing members and by providing a space in which to define itself. Simply appearing in and being labeled by the media affords groups the opportunity to become part of the political and cultural scene. In a movement's formative years, the news media can be *constitutive,* defining and establishing the movement not only for the public but for the group's current and potential members as well (Armstrong, 2002). In this way, too, backlash from opposition groups can grant visibility and raise awareness for social and identity movements. For example, in 1977 celebrity singer

Anita Bryant launched the hateful "Save the Children" campaign in Miami, Florida, one of the first political coalition groups organized against the gay rights movement. Bryant's campaign successfully overturned an equal rights ordinance that would have protected gays and lesbians from discrimination in housing and employment opportunities, on the grounds that the law would prohibit schools from teaching morality. Bryant's anti-gay crusade won, as 70 percent of Dade County voters voted to repeal the ordinance. However, the increased press attention surrounding the controversy ultimately contributed to the growth of the gay identity movement. "By recognizing and publicizing gay identity, Bryant participated in creating her enemy. In cultural struggles like this one, all press is, in a sense, good press. By generating media coverage the backlash further disseminated gay identity and the gay rights agenda" (Armstrong, 2002, p. 128).

Arguably, however, the contemporary gay rights movement is in a different position. Its dependency on media attention has greatly diminished, as much of the movement's political work does not necessitate "the media's gaze" (Carroll & Ratner, 1999). No longer requiring press attention to mobilize and attract members, many gay rights groups take a more cautious stance toward media publicity. As my interviews indicate, many within the movement are critical of those groups that "gain visibility by becoming the exotic objects of heterosexist media copy" (Carroll & Ratner, 1999, p. 20).

As a corrective to the media "freak show" in which groups like ACT UP (AIDS Coalition to Unleash Power) perform a "spectacle" for the television news cameras, many of today's movement leaders craft communication strategies with straight allies, ones that are directed toward straight audiences, in an effort to normalize and mainstream gay and lesbian life. As this next section highlights, most activists were initially resistant to even talking about the "m word" in the mainstream media.

The Struggle from Within: Making Marriage Matter

I was curious early on in this project about how social actors in identity politics come to organize around and highlight one particular goal—in this case, achieving equal marriage rights—over others. News reporting on the issue presented same-sex marriage as "the" gay interest—constructing a mass movement united by one homogenous goal, often reducing gay activism to a single-issue cause. But the same media coverage that stressed marriage as emblematic of gay activism in general also worked to silence the internal struggle over marriage that has been at the center of debate within the gay community. As Roberta Sklar of the Task Force explained, "If we are forced by the dominant culture to deal with many of these family recognition issues under the umbrella of marriage, then we will . . . We as an organization have never put our eggs in any one basket, and we're not putting it in the marriage basket. We wrangle at the fact that we've been pushed by societal pressures to look at all these things under that umbrella, but we won't adhere to that in a rigid way."

A relatively new issue, marriage equality was not a major goal of gay political activism until the mid-1990s, as groups failed to find consensus over the marriage issue and were focused on what many activists considered to be more pressing concerns—namely, "HIV and health care, AIDS prevention, the repeal of sodomy laws, anti-gay violence, job discrimination, immigration, media coverage, military antigay policy, sex inequality, and the saturation of everyday life by heterosexual privilege" (Warner, 1999, p. 84). Gay marriage was not a part of early political activist efforts, mostly because marriage laws by their very nature were opposed to the basic tenets of what the gay movement historically stood for: the state regulation of sexuality.

Recognizing the historical tensions over the marriage issue from within the gay community, my analysis in this section shows how, for the most part, gay rights activists did not proactively pursue a battle over marriage rights. These informants fully recognized the risks of bringing gay marriage into the realm of mainstream political debate and public discourse but nonetheless felt that avoiding the issue would hinder progress on a wide variety of LGBT issues.

My own entry into this project naively assumed a proactive, organized effort on the part of gay rights activists to push same-sex marriage onto the public and media agendas. To some extent, some of the smaller single-issue groups that were organized specifically around marriage did actively seek to do battle on the marriage front. But it became almost instantaneously clear during the interview process that for most activists, especially those who were with the larger, multi-issue gay rights organizations, same-sex marriage was not a battle of choice, but one they were forced to contend with due to pressures from conservative right opponents—and fought begrudgingly in the arena of the mainstream media.

Activists commonly referred to their position in the debate as "playing defense," claiming that marriage "was not a battle of our choosing." Evoking the metaphor of a skirmish that breaks out at a school playground, one informant described the gay movement as being the smaller, weaker kid who is perpetually picked on and eventually has to stand up for himself. As Roberta explained, "When a bully kicks you in the teeth, and you don't fight back, they know they can kick you over and over and over again. So it's critical for the little guy to get up and do something and say, 'you are not going to be able to do this to me! Even if my mouth is bleeding, you are not going to be able to kick me in the teeth again!'"

Continuing the analogy of a stronger, tougher, more organized enemy bullying gay rights proponents, Chris of the Log Cabin Republicans argued, "They [social conservatives] talk about the gay agenda forcing this issue, when really, we were simply reacting to the right-wing agenda." Similarly, Michael, communications director for the Human Rights Campaign, explained, "marriage interestingly enough came to prominence not because of our community but because of our opponents."

In his estimation, conservatives sensed defeat after the 2003 *Lawrence v. Texas* decision when the U.S. Supreme Court repealed anti-sodomy laws, seen as a landmark victory for the gay and lesbian rights movement. Fearing that *Lawrence* might pave the way for legalizing more rights for gay and lesbian citizens (including marriage), conservative groups in a retaliatory and preemptive move began to push state-by-state for constitutional amendments that would "shut the door on marriage equality as much as possible." Conservative groups sensed they could use the gay marriage controversy for political gain, rally constituents around the issue, and fire up their core base. My activist informants did not necessarily credit conservative opponents with *creating* the issue, but argued that "they propelled this into the national spotlight in a way that was not our community's doing" (Michael, Human Rights Campaign).

Taken further, according to many activists, the gay marriage debate was a diabolical political strategy crafted by the Bush administration. Conservative strategists worked to construct gay people as the modern equivalent of "the boogie man," as they have historically done, and to benefit politically by scapegoating an already disenfranchised group. This sentiment is reflected in the words of one informant who describes a conspiratorial strategy on the part of the Bush administration, painting a picture of White House staff sitting around a conference room conjuring up ways to win the next election.

Karl Rove's agenda was to say, look, I've got a president who's going into his reelection cycle. He's not all that strong. I've got a war that I can't quite explain. I've got an economy I haven't been able to turn around. I've got 45 million Americans without health insurance. I've got an education system that's still got all the same problems it had. Hmmm . . . How are we going to get our base revved up and that little core middle we've got to pull over, to get our 51 percent distracted enough to not ask us the tough questions like deficits and balanced budgets? I know, we'll talk about gay marriage! And you know, candidates have been campaigning forever on fear strategies. And Reagan, it was the Cold War . . . Bush, its 9/11 and those gay people, we're coming to get you! (Cheryl, former president and executive director of the Human Rights Campaign)

So while the marriage conversation took on a new life after the *Lawrence* and *Goodridge* decisions, it was when the Bush administration made the issue part of the 2004 presidential campaign that gay rights activists universally said they had to "reshuffle the deck" and turn more organizational resources and attention toward marriage. Activists anticipated the right-wing response to the historic *Goodridge* case (legalizing same-sex marriage in Massachusetts) to be vehement. But movement leaders said they were shocked when the president went before Congress and asked representatives to amend the U.S. Constitution to limit marriage to one man and one woman. Cheryl, then president of the Human Rights Campaign (HRC), recalls her reaction to the president's call for the Federal Marriage Amendment (FMA), a move that pushed gay marriage from the periphery to the center. "The president took to the airwaves in February calling for the passage of the Federal Marriage Amendment. Now, this is a president who holds very few news conferences, and he held an emergency news conference, saying the most pressing matter before the American public is those gay people, and we better get that Federal Marriage Amendment passed or else! Talk about catapulting it and convincing people there's some sort of emergency here and the sky is falling." The aftermath of the *Goodridge* decision and the process of being thrown into the center of mainstream presidential politics forced gay rights organizations to shift priorities in order to dedicate increased energy, resources, and messaging to marriage. Seth, who was elevated to a new position of vice president of the Marriage Project for the HRC as a result of this increased public attention, recalled, "I've never actually seen an organization as big as this one turn so quickly to make an issue a political priority." As the national LGBT organization that works primarily on Capitol Hill, they "reshuffled resources relatively quickly" to make sure that the FMA was defeated.

Coming to the decision to foreground the marriage issue was, in Seth's view, not mired in controversy, but was rather "surprisingly tension-free." In other words, it became obvious to organizational leaders that they had to allocate the resources to protect the *Goodridge* decision, defeat the FMA, and build a political climate state-by-state that would support marriage equality. But with limited funds, resources, and staff, turning to focus on one priority meant that time and attention was invariably taken from others. Michael, who at the time worked as the HRC's communications specialist (by the time of the later interview period, he had become the director of communication), explains how shifting political priorities toward marriage led to organizational strains.

> It [marriage] was an issue that we obviously spent less time and resources on, because while that does equal full equality, there are so many other issues and things in this country where LGBT people are denied, you know, their right

to a job. Because in 34 states you can still be fired for being gay or lesbian. In 44 states you can be fired for being transgender in this country. So there are workplace issues, there are hate crimes issues, there's access to HIV/AIDS prevention and treatment. It's not that we are ever at a loss of issues to deal with. But the marriage conversation has required us to focus in more closely on relationship recognition.

In a subsequent interview, the former president of the HRC indicated that shifting institutional priorities and resources to marriage was contentious, the center of an "unresolvable conflict" that eventually led to her departure soon after the defeats of the 2004 election. In her estimation, marriage was never a goal of the organization, at least not at the level that it should have been. She criticized her former organization, and the national movement more generally, for *reacting* to the *Goodridge* victory. In her view the unanticipated success in the legislative arena caught gay rights leaders off guard, forcing the messaging arm of the movement to play catch-up. Criticizing the defensive posture and the lack of preparedness on the part of the movement, she said the marriage win created organizational pains of having to scramble for resources. The leaders at her organization were "not celebrating the passage of *Goodridge* and embracing it; they're saying [sighs], 'Oh, shit, now that it's here, I guess we better fight this good fight.'"

Leaders of the nation's largest gay rights organization weren't the only ones with cold feet. As her words reflect, the resistance, fear, and hesitance over marriage that Cheryl described within her former organization was indicative of a tension felt on a larger scale within the gay and lesbian community. Evan, considered by many to be the father of the modern movement for marriage equality, spoke at length about the internal debates over marriage that were waged long before the victory in Massachusetts. His work on marriage began in the 1980s when he worked pro bono on behalf of gay couples wanting to marry. At that time, he described his camp of pro-marriage supporters within the LGBT activist community as a "small minority."

Resistance within the gay community came from those who were opposed to marriage based on ideological grounds and tactical grounds. The ideological camp was opposed to fighting for marriage because they didn't like what the institution represented, feeling marriage was too narrow in scope. As one activist explained, some members felt like "instead we ought to be talking about more broadly challenging family structure or . . . the way our society provides protections and benefits and so on." The other category of resistance among activists were people who, regardless of their ideological position, felt that marriage would be a strategic failure for the movement as a whole. As Evan explained, some activists were concerned "that the fight for the freedom to marry was either premature or potentially dangerous. That it would trigger a crackdown, a greater reaction, an opposition."

This fear of engendering a stronger response from opponents led to internal frictions about whether to move forward with the *Goodridge* legal case. Many feared the case was premature and that a victory would be the "longest of shots." The co-chair of the Massachusetts Gay and Lesbian Political Caucus, a lobbying group that works in the state legislature, called her organization "one of the last holdouts" on the marriage front. She pleaded with the GLAD legal team to delay the *Goodridge* lawsuit because "we knew that people weren't ready for it. We knew that if they filed the lawsuit there would be an immediate backlash."

Leaders at GLAD were acutely aware of the risks of catapulting marriage into legal, political, and cultural debate. As Carisa, communications director for GLAD, explained, the team eventually took the case despite resistance from others in the movement. "It's part of the agenda because there was a demand for it, not because there was necessarily a leadership that decided that it was a top agenda item." Mary, a civil rights attorney at GLAD, tells the story of when she started as a lawyer 15 years ago, one of the first phone calls she received was from a couple who wanted to get married. According to Carisa, Mary had told her that "for a good 11 years, she [Mary] received phone calls like that from people who wanted help getting married. And she told people, 'No, now is not the time.' That there are these other sorts of legal, political, and social building blocks that need to be in place first."

For most activists, then, the "m word" was not only dangerous but also utterly inconceivable. The community was acutely aware of the explosive potential of pushing the marriage agenda. One informant explained why, with the exception of a couple of pioneering individuals like Evan, the activist community was slow to embrace marriage. "For most activists, it was so unattainable. They didn't dare to dream about marriage. It wasn't that they didn't want it, it wasn't that they wouldn't have articulated it as a goal. They never believed they could get there . . . the prejudice and the hate were so strong and the demonization of gay people was so strong that you would never expect normal social acceptance in a cultural arena like the right to marry."

The divide within the movement over whether to pursue equal marriage ultimately gave birth to new organizations and new sorts of activists who were disappointed with "the gay establishment's" fear of the issue. Some splintered off to start their own activist work or began building independent single-issue organizations dedicated solely to marriage equality. For example, two of my informants for this study left larger gay rights organizations, the Human Rights Campaign and Lambda Legal, because they wanted to work exclusively on marriage. For leaders in these organizations, the issue rose to the agenda not because activists dreamed it up, nor because the opposition pushed the controversy, but because marriage rights were something gay people had been wanting for a long time. While working pro bono at Lambda for couples who wanted help getting married, Evan argued that it was the desire of gay couples, not necessarily activists, that drove legal organizations to bring forth cases even "without the blessing of . . . the gay establishment."

At least one of these informants joined the fight and started her own organization, Marriage Equality USA, because of her personal desire to marry her partner. Davina, whose story is featured in the introduction of this book, described how her desire to marry her partner, Molly, overcame the resistance she felt from those in her own community. "In the early years, in '98, when we were doing stuff around marriage, a lot of people within the LGBT community were like, 'Why are you focused on this? That's really not our issue.' Or, 'That's so far away, you're not being realistic.' But we [Molly and I] still really wanted to get married." The act of participating in a ritualized ceremony transformed Davina and her partner from merely a couple who wanted to marry to activists entrenched in the movement for marriage equality. The ceremony they had with friends and family in 1998 convinced them "that this was something we wanted to work towards as a couple because it was the right thing to do. Because we loved each other. We saw, just having the ceremony, we did tons of education. Going to order a cake. Getting the rings. Or renting a place."

She went on to describe what characterizes the people involved in Marriage Equality USA as different from the other national gay and lesbian organizations. Their members, activists, and board members are entirely made up of people just like her, who want to get married themselves and are not necessarily tied to the larger gay and lesbian movement. They are employed outside the movement and do their activist work on the side. At times, she explained, these activists felt disconnected from the larger political aims of gay and lesbian movement. Her comment about the generational divide highlights the competing political logics of the gay liberation movement, centered on the critical view of social institutions like marriage, and the assimilationist logic of the contemporary gay rights movement. As Davina explained:

> Our main activities are not in working with the LGBT community. So we come at it at a much more grassroots level. We haven't been privy to the politics, the years of politics. I grew up in a different generation. The generation above me was pretty anti-marriage to begin with. It was sort of more of the feminist, sexual liberation movement that was more interested in tearing down the patriarchy, tearing down institutions, and being able to experience sexual liberation . . . I didn't have that same thing when I was growing up. It's like, we feel like we want to be able to be a part of the fabric of society, not the fringe.

Even among people who actively sought marriage rights on the behalf of couples, they understood the risks of going mainstream with an issue as explosive as gay marriage. But their attempts to avoid the issue were thwarted by a political opposition hungry to do battle over marriage and a commercial media system eager to air that debate over a hot-button issue. As Evan explained, even if a gay rights debate revolved around other measures entirely, marriage would inevitably come up. "Try as hard as we might, those of us in the legal organizations, activists, and so on, to find ways of challenging discrimination without tackling the exclusion to marriage, time and time again, we would run up against the exclusion to marriage being offered as a justification for discrimination." He tells the story of his own entry into the media landscape as a gay rights spokesperson, illustrating the centrality of the media as constitutive of the marriage debate:

> My very first national television appearance as a gay activist was on *Crossfire*, and I was on because then Mayor Koch of New York City had issued an executive order allowing for bereavement leave for city employees. You know, this is at the height of the AIDS epidemic. And it was a minimal humane measure to allow gay couples, gay survivors, to grieve their partners.
>
> So I go on the show, and [my opponent] immediately starts attacking me, saying what he wants is gay marriage. And I would have to say, "Yes, actually I do think gay people should have the freedom to marry, but that's not what this is about. This is about a very modest, very minimal, very merely humane and decent measure allowing people to grieve their loss." And I thought to myself, if we're going to have this fight over marriage anyway, even when we're thinking something so minimal, why shouldn't we fight for everything we deserve?

As Evan's narrative of his induction as a national media spokesperson reveals, the mainstream news media was critical in pushing the marriage issue front and center in cultural politics. The intense media frenzy that continued over same-sex-marriage rights created an increased need for institutional strategic communications within these activist organizations. When the marriage debate began to dominate media coverage of gay and lesbian life, leaders in the movement began to see the issue as an opportunity to reform representations of their community.

Producing Gay Marriage for the Mainstream

The cultural fascination with same-sex marriages turned the media eye on gay and lesbian issues in unprecedented ways. Carisa, who had worked for decades on a host of gay rights issues from military inclusion to AIDS advocacy to employment nondiscrimination, put it this way: "Marriage has become this juggernaut. It's taken on this life in popular culture. I would predict there would never be another issue like it, that's gay related, that's had sort of the saturation coverage that marriage has had." As the communications director for the Task Force pointed out, her job was no longer about visibility, but about controlling the messaging. "Ten years ago, when I was working on the New York State issues, we had to battle to get gay issues into the press. Today we have to compete to get your message and the way you want it framed into the press. Because pick up on any given day the top ten newspapers in the country, and there will probably be eight stories related to something that is about the gay community."

This shift from merely being recognized by the mainstream media to controlling the framing of issues led to organizational restructuring, so most of the large national activist organizations required a communications director or similar position to manage media inquiries and strategies. In fact, several of these public relations and communications professionals I spoke with were new to their positions in 2004 and 2005, hired in response to the increased media attention surrounding the marriage issue. As several informants explained, they had been hired because the organization had to "beef up" its communications capacity and public education efforts due to press inquiries about gay marriage. The coverage surrounding the San Francisco mayor's issuance of marriage licenses alone was astounding, even for activists who had worked on messaging for decades. One activist, who had been a national media spokesperson for the gay rights movement for over 20 years, explained, "When Newsom issued marriage licenses, the coverage of that was just beyond anything I'd ever seen before on any gay issue before. I mean, you had 60 satellite trucks in front of city hall and you had outlets from Bogota, Colombia, to South Korea news, to obviously everything in between and all the national mainstream media. It was a fabulous human interest story. This whole city was electrified."

Events like these placed an increased burden on organizations to develop and fund a communications department that could build a strategic communications plan, hire and train professionals to answer media inquiries, create a bank of sources, conduct research about media coverage, and develop credible spokespeople to represent the organization.

The media attention changed the nature of even litigation groups like GLAD, whose purpose was once to keep controversial cases below the radar of the press, doing battle in the courtroom rather than in the court of public opinion. But the increased visibility of gay and lesbian issues, and the weight of the marriage issue specifically, forced GLAD to expand in such a way that a case like *Goodridge* became not just about the legal court maneuvering but about public communications tactics as well. According to the communications director of GLAD, the case was packaged within a carefully crafted communications strategy that undeniably influenced the selection of the seven plaintiff couples who were chosen by the organization to represent gay marriage. As the litigation was being planned, "there was a communication strategy around it. I think certainly, who the plaintiffs were, and how they presented publicly, and their sort of likeableness and attractiveness and articulateness and all of that stuff, made a big difference."

The anticipated media circus weighed heavily on the minds of those planning the historic and controversial case that ultimately legalized gay marriage in Massachusetts. The plaintiff couples were carefully selected by this litigation group to appeal to a mainstream audience to appear pleasant, sympathetic, and palatable. Being media savvy was a prerequisite for selection. In order to be represented by the group and in front of television news cameras, these couples had to already be "out" in all aspects of their lives (for example, out at work and with other family members) and have the sort of flexible occupations that allowed them to attend media trainings, press conferences, and hearings. As discussed in chapter 4, in 2004 these conditions inadvertently limited the racial, ethnic, and class diversity of the couples selected.

News exposure of the *Goodridge* case and the San Francisco weddings transported visual images of gays and lesbians getting married into the living rooms of Middle America. The debate was no longer talking heads musing about what *might* happen if gays could marry. Americans were turning on nightly news programs and witnessing for themselves gays and lesbians getting married in San Francisco, New York, Oregon, and Massachusetts. Those already working in communications departments had to turn their attention almost entirely to crafting appropriate narratives about marriage equality.

Activists sensed that marriage was their ticket in; it was what would allow them to talk about their issues with prominent news entities and reach national news audiences. But the focus on marriage limited the conversation as well. One activist who appeared as a spokesperson on a wide variety of network and cable news programs pointedly explained, "*NBC Nightly News* doesn't call you to talk about the employment nondiscrimination act. You're lucky if you can get a word in edgewise that they don't edit out. Marriage, they want to talk about marriage. Why? Because it's the hot issue." Other causes important to the movement that were "not-so-hot" took a backseat to marriage, or at least had to be framed within the larger context of relationship recognition.

But from the perspective of most activists, this shift in attention to marriage in no way replaced or competed with other issues such as violence against gays and lesbians and access to HIV treatment, but it gave them a "larger microphone" to talk about equality for LGBT citizens more broadly. Deflecting complaints waged by others in the movement that marriage unfairly dominates the agenda and overshadows other important causes, the former head of HRC explained, "People would say to me, 'How did marriage become priority number one? What about job discrimination?' And I would say, it's all intertwined. It's all inter-tangled. It's all part of the same equality vocabulary. But marriage is the buzzword, because that's what the press and the politicians are all talking about. They're not talking about job discrimination for gay people; they're just buzzing about gay marriage." As Evan explained it, marriage does not limit the conversation, but rather opens the door to talking about a whole host of issues by affording a kind of legitimacy and social status previously unknown to the gay and lesbian community.

> Marriage is a vocabulary in which . . . people talk about who you are and define who you are. And therefore claiming that vocabulary and helping people see our lives in this vocabulary of love of caring and dedication and commitment and so on would transform the position of gay people in a way that would then benefit us on a variety of other battles that we would also be fighting. In other words, winning marriage is not the only thing that matters. But talking about our lives in the vocabulary of marriage would help us win better protection against bullying for kids in schools, better treatments with regards to AIDS, access to health care and so on.

But despite the best intentions of activists to use marriage to discuss other issues that are critical to the gay rights movement, including access to health care, employment nondiscrimination, the diversity of their community, and AIDS funding, media analysis shows the news agenda centered universally on the gay marriage issue, discussing other issues only within the context of relationship recognition (see discussion in chapters 3 and 4).

Appearing in the news media under the umbrella of marriage gave the community opportunities to present themselves as "normal"—as couples in loving, monogamous relationships, as nurturing parents, as individuals yearning to build a family life. These images are boundary-breaking considering the historic representation of LGBT people as predatory villains, promiscuous perverts, laughable buffoons, and queer radicals—essentially, the culturally constructed "antithesis" of wholesome family values.

As comments from informants indicated, although many may have been initially hesitant to do battle on the marriage front in the mass media, in the end they welcomed the marriage conversation as a way to reform the images they had seen of themselves in the press and popular culture. Consistent with other marginalized groups, researchers have traced coverage of the LGBT community, once virtually nonexistent, as moving from invisibility to one that perpetuated anti-gay stereotypes (Alwood, 1996; Bennet, 2000; Gross, 2001; Gross & Woods, 1999). Gay rights activists in this study were keenly aware of these patterns of representation, as well as how such depictions would undermine the position of gay people by offending the sensibilities of a heterosexist culture. Informants feared what these exoticized images might signify, captured in comments like this one from Cheryl:

> Twenty or some years ago, gay people were portrayed as deviants, perverts, sexually obsessed. Public's image of a gay person was what they saw at a gay pride [parade], some woman walking down the street naked, some guy . . . half naked or dressed half like a woman. And you'd be like, "Oh, shit, like a freak show." "I don't want my kids to see this, this is scary." "I don't want them living next to me." I mean, it was just terrible for everyone, including people like me. That's not who I am, and I'm gay.

Informants struggled to separate themselves from what they perceived to be the more "radical" paraders who had appeared on the nightly news for so many years by practicing performative media strategies. These assimilatory media strategies were part of an overall policy to build programs that were directed toward what my activist informants referred to as their "straight allies." An integral part of the organizational strategy was to build an alliance of gay and non-gay organizations and to construct same-sex marriage as "not just a gay issue," but one tied to universal concerns of economic justice and workplace nondiscrimination. These organizations worked to build alliances with labor unions like the American Federation of Labor and Congress of Industrial Organizations (AFL-CIO), civil rights organizations like the National Association for the Advancement of Colored People (NAACP), and human rights groups like the American Civil Liberties Union (ACLU). Employing a common civil rights discourse, one activist explained the need for non-gay alliances in this way: "There is no movement against oppression by any minority that has been able to be achieved without the support of the majority. If you only had black abolitionists, we'd still be living in slavery right now."

Activists strategically crafted narratives about gay marriage and about gay life that would highlight alliances with non-gay partners and resonate with mainstream audiences—messages that would "play in Peoria," as the saying goes, or connect with Middle America. As one informant who works for the national Republican gay and lesbian organization told me point-blank, same-sex marriage is not a radical anti-family movement as defined by his own party. It is a "conservative fight," part of the struggle to win the "battle to be boring." Employing discourses that are popular among gay conservatives asserting that marriage would "tame the wild beast" of homosexual love (Walters, 2001b), he argued that the gay movement and society more generally should embrace same-sex marriage because it encourages gays to enter long-term, monogamous relationships.

As comments from these informants indicate, activists on the marriage front used two symbiotic discursive strategies to, on the one hand, construct gay and lesbian life as normal, banal, and ordinary, and, on the other, to differentiate themselves from the "freak show" imagery of drag queens and proud paraders that had been the predominant visual imagery of LGBT communities in the news. Critical to this strategy was to separate themselves from a gay movement that is seen as radical, separatist, and defiant. These informants sought to depoliticize gay identity in an effort to normalize gay marriage. In the following comment from Cheryl, the historic battle cry of the gay identity movement appears almost obsolete and powerless in helping with the daily concerns of average middle-class gay Americans: "This isn't about trying to get your parish priests to sanction our relationship, because we need that, you know, 'We're here, we're queer, we want it in your face.' This is about me worrying about Jen [my partner] and the kids if I get killed, and will she end up losing the house? And my kids won't go to college because she can't figure out how to support our kids?"

Concerned that the news media was constructing gay marriages as "radical" and threatening to mainstream values, my activist informants were critical of the kinds of images news crews shot of gay and lesbian life. Activists who worked intimately with the news media were acutely aware of the power of images and how these pictures of their community might contribute to public perceptions. Early in the debate, organizations began to track how gays and lesbians were being depicted in the news, paying careful attention to what is referred to as the "b-roll," the standard use of images and full-motion video that accompany the journalistic narration in television news stories. As one communications director for the HRC explained, "When news stories are produced about our community, it's the b-roll of images, what goes under the voice-over, that paints a picture of who you're talking about." They discovered a predictable pattern of images that accompanied nearly every news story about gay people that ran on television—even same-sex marriage stories—of showing anonymous and generally faceless individuals in gay bars. He discussed in detail how this visual framing worked to create a storyline of who gay people are:

> So you have this view: gay people apparently like to drink a lot or are in these dark, seedy places often shown the backs of their heads, not showing their faces. Because there was this interest in protecting people's anonymity. But at the same time, if all you're seeing is the backs of people's heads it leads you to

believe that they're ashamed to show their faces. So there is that shame ele-ment to it. Or people walking down the street always from the back, sometimes the most gratuitous displays of public affection they could get on camera. So while most gay people aren't walking down the street making out, that makes for "good television."

He argued with news media personnel that it was inaccurate and irresponsible to, for example, cover the *Goodridge* case with these stock b-roll images:"This is about two women and their daughter and them seeking protections; why would you show video of some guys in a bar to represent their life?"

Frustrated with the stock of video images used by local and national tele-vision outlets to tell the story of gay marriage, this gay rights organization shot and disseminated video clips for news outlets to use as b-roll, a practice common in public relations. These images were used to strategically construct their own original visual narratives of gay life as a corrective to the staple diet of bar life imagery. To visually support coverage of the *Goodridge* case in Massachusetts, for example, they shot b-roll of the plaintiff couples, crafting a narrative of normalcy and everyday banality. Images included couples walking their dog, cooking dinner, coming home from work, and playing Monopoly with their kids, "all of those things that are what families do but are so entirely different than those images that you had been seeing" (Michael, Human Rights Campaign). They provided the video images to local and national media outlets and were pleased to see that the b-roll was picked up and used.

Activists in the marriage movement contrasted these everyday images of coupledom with what they described as the more common and less desir-able footage of "mass" gay ceremonies. As chapter 3 details, news entities frequently shot footage showing hordes of anonymous same-sex couples standing in long lines that wrapped around city blocks, waiting outside city hall in places like San Francisco. Other activists complained of dated stock footage of mass weddings that included same-sex couples in a field dressed in traditional wedding garb to protest their exclusion from marriage. These images of mass weddings troubled informants, because they did not look like "the real thing" or fully represent the more "traditional" ceremonies many same-sex couples opt for. Activists wanted to avoid circus-like ceremonial imagery that looked more like a performative public display rather than an intimate and meaningful ritual. One informant discussed the problematic images that were replayed from a protest event on the mall in Washington, D.C., in the early 1990s: "And you see this over and over, two women in dresses kissing or two men in tuxedos or two women in tuxedos. And it has this sort of circus-like atmosphere to it that also, I think, does a disservice to couples who have very sort of traditional ceremonies. But then people associate . . . gay marriage . . . wedding . . . this wedding is this 10,000 people thing with crazy outfits. What is that? It doesn't feel like marriage to them" (Michael, Human Rights Campaign).

Paradoxically, some informants even seemed reluctant to celebrate coverage of a milestone moment for marriage equality: the controversial gesture by San Francisco mayor Gavin Newsom to grant marriage licenses to same-sex couples in February 2004. There was concern that video images panning long lines of couples waiting to marry were a spectacle that "could turn some people off," making gay wedding ceremonies look more like "people waiting in line to get tickets to a rock concert." As one communications director put it bluntly, "This is not Mardi Gras."

The communications director for GLAD talked about their organization's specific strategies to separate themselves from the spectacle of the San Francisco weddings, which she defined as "extra legal." It was an important aspect of their communications strategy to define the Massachusetts weddings as legal "real marriages" that could not be rescinded rather than merely "symbolic" media events. In preparing for the *Goodridge* case, then, she said, "There was a lot of planning around presenting these marriages as mainstream. So on the day it became possible for people to marry, May 17, there was a great deal of planning around the weddings of the seven couples. And giving media people access to them. And showing people being embraced by their families, and their communities, and their religions, getting married. It wasn't pictures of people on the steps on city hall in San Francisco, where it was more of a carnival atmosphere."

Implicit in this struggle to "sell" marriage to the mainstream was a fundamental disagreement among those in the movement about how to frame marriage in the early stages of public debate—employing either discourses of love or discourses of equal rights. In this next section, I show how the movement split over these competing definitional strategies—whether to define marriage as a package of rights and responsibilities or as the ultimate expression of love and commitment.

For Love or Money: Competing Definitional Discourses

In 2005, when I asked my informants why they believed gay and lesbian people should fight for marriage equality, they began reciting a common script—one I heard repeated time and again with amazing consistency—recounting a long list of rights, benefits, and protections that are afforded exclusively through the institution of marriage. Informants spoke of the 1,138 federal protections, such as family medical leave, hospital visitation rights, inheritance, social security benefits, pensions, and federal tax policy, in addition to the state and local policies that reward marriage participants.

Describing these rights, informants framed the institution within economic concerns of financial security and stability, the "bread-and-butter kitchen table issues" that families deal with day to day. Economic concerns were used to differentiate marriage from other less desirable forms of relationship recognition like domestic partnerships and civil unions. Using these rights discourses, informants immediately began talking about marriage as a set of *financial* benefits—tied closely to notions of stability, security, and emotional peace of mind—for gay and lesbian families and communities. Some activists spoke of their own relationships in this way, feeling personally burdened by financial worries because of their exclusion from marriage. As Cheryl explained, "As a family, I live in fear . . . I mean, I try to financially plan for it. I'm more precautious about savings. Because I know if I die in a plane trip Thursday going home, I leave [my partner] Jen with a big mortgage, two children. I don't know how she works and does child care, and no support through my social security program because they won't recognize her."

Not surprisingly, the equal rights frame directed the overall media strategy that most organizations relied upon to tell their stories about marriage, revolving around the legal and financial repercussions of being excluded from marriage. These communications and public relations professionals told "heartbreaking stories" that would reach various cohorts and appeal to gay and non-gay constituencies. Informants sought to capitalize on the limited resources and deadline pressures journalists face and condensed their marriage stories into neat, press-friendly packages. Activists categorized specific media stories they would cycle through—for example, "the kids story" and "the seniors story"—to provide the news media with "fresh meat" that would keep reporters interested in new angles.

For example, informants packaged "the kids story" as focusing on the child of a gay or lesbian couple who becomes sick and is unable to receive treatment because she is not covered under her biological mom's health insurance plan. Likewise, activists told the story of Annie (and others like her), the child of Hillary and Julie Goodridge, who lacked the emotional and financial security of knowing her parents were married and desperately wanted to be just like any other family. Whatever the specific details, the underlying message of the kids narrative is, as one activist bluntly put it, "Even if you hate us, don't screw [over] our children."

Another successful narrative that ended up being a "gold mine," according to one activist, was the story of the elderly gay or lesbian couple. The "seniors story" was successful as a strategy for lobbying legislators and was appealing to journalists, since most people already sympathize with the elderly population. A familiar seniors narrative would be about a couple who had built a life together for decades (30 to 50 years). When one partner dies, the other is left essentially homeless because, unprotected from federal tax policy, she cannot afford the taxes on the house. The seniors story was popular among reporters and news audiences alike because it was coded with symbolic meanings about what gay and lesbian life looked like. Like children, seniors are "cute and cuddly," in the words of Arlene, desexualized and therefore nonthreatening. Additionally, these stories involved "super-stable" gay or lesbian couples whose relationships had lasted longer than most heterosexual marriages.

These stories—kids and seniors—were the successful ones, the ones that journalists and editors "ate up," the ones that appealed to a wide audience. They were stories about treating people equally and providing society's most vulnerable populations with security and basic human rights. There were other stories activists tried to tell, however—stories about the economic and racial diversity of their community, stories about religious tolerance, stories about the consequences of marriage exclusion for international couples— that were more challenging to tell and ultimately failed to garner or sustain media interest. Even when stories were successful, activists faced yet another problem when reporters began to tire of these same framing strategies. "It got to a point, the press would say to me, 'Yeah, yeah, yeah, the senior story, Arlene. We've already covered it already. Yeah, yeah, yeah, kids. I know kids. You've done kids. What else do you have there?'"

As coverage became more intense, communications strategists in the movement felt the demand to create new ways to tell stories about marriage and family. This ultimately gave way to competing definitional strategies, a core divide in the movement over how best to characterize and symbolize the meaning of marriage—as a package of rights or as the ultimate expression of romantic love. As represented in the comments below, although many activists saw these two tactics at odds with one other, both had the same goal: to appeal to the "moveable middle."

While many in the movement thought framing marriage as a package of legal and financial rights would resonate most successfully with mass audiences, the head of the Marriage Project for the Human Rights Campaign began to have his doubts. In his estimation this strategy was failing. Research from polling and focus groups conducted by the organization demonstrated that the straight audiences they were supposedly reaching didn't think of marriage in those terms. He explained:

If you ask a typical non-gay couple, "Why did you get married?" they don't immediately go to, "Well, so I can get tax breaks and make sure that I can see my partner in the hospital" . . . I think we need now to take those legalistic arguments and create more empathy . . . We need the average voter and average American to think of our relationships the same way they think of their own: you get married because you love the person you want to get married to. That's why you get married.

These informants defined marriage not as a set of "unemotional" rights, obligations, and responsibilities, but as universal and humanizing "romantic love." Activists invoked love as the common language for understanding marriage, and marriage as the common language to define relationships in society. The communications director for GLAD described "love and commitment" as a competing discourse to the predominant "rights" language that had defined marriage for many in the movement. Her statement demonstrates the attempt to appeal to straight allies by characterizing romantic love as the universal social language:

I think the main theme [surrounding the *Goodridge* case] was about love and commitment rather than being about rights. That these are people who love each other. These are people who have built a life together and are committed to each other, and that marriage is the ultimate adult expression of that kind of commitment . . . Straight people say, "Oh, my God, they deserve it. They've been together for 30 years. If you can still stand each other, you definitely deserve to get married." It's a common language. It's a shared language.

Another activist who managed the public education efforts at Freedom to Marry demonstrated how talking about marriage solely as a package of rights erases the emotional "true meaning" of marriage: "You don't propose to someone, you know, 'Would you like to share my health insurance? Would you like to have equal rights to own a home with me?' It's about love. It's about commitment. It's about heart."

Other activists pointed out how the terms surrounding marriage, terms like "wedding," "husband," "wife," and "spouse," come with a certain degree of social weightiness, credibility, and cultural acceptance. They are terms that are relational, unconditional, and require no explanation, as opposed to the more legal terms associated with gay marriage, like "domestic partner." As one activist commented, a domestic partner sounds like someone who cleans your house rather than someone with whom you build a life.

These activists who sought to talk about marriage within discourses of love argued that rights language was not only unappealing to mainstream audiences but also potentially problematic. From their research, they found that public opinion polls indicated that Americans respond negatively to rights and "entitlement" language, especially when it concerns gay people and other minority groups. As Carisa of GLAD explained, Americans see rights as competitive and oppositional, so if one particular marginalized group is awarded rights, then their own group's rights are inherently taken away. In this way granting same-sex couples equal marriage is seen as handing down "special rights," a framing strategy disseminated by social conservatives asserting that these equal rights represent something "extra" extended to an already privileged group.

But for activists who highlighted a rights discourse, talking about marriage as romantic love was far more hazardous. It not only sexualized gay and lesbian relationships; it also asked heterosexuals to recognize and accept them as equals. These activists struggled to keep the messaging of marriage "on track" by talking only about rights. One activist who lobbied for gay rights in the Massachusetts legislature complained about other groups in the movement attempting to assert a love discourse, undoing any progress they were making to gain rights on a variety of issues. "If you're going to talk about marriage at all—and please don't—the last thing you should do is talk about recognition. The law is not created as a form of therapy to make us feel better about our relationships. They will resent it, and it will never sell. Who gives a damn whether they recognize us or not? We want rights, we want benefits, we want to be treated equally, regardless of what they think of us."

Among those who wanted to define marriage solely as rights was a fear that packaging marriage as romantic love would only contribute further to the "ick factor," the term commonly used to refer to straight culture's repulsion to homosexual sex acts. Since romantic discourses and wedding imagery might sexualize gay and lesbian relationships, leaders of the Massachusetts Gay and Lesbian Political Caucus coached couples to leave their wedding albums at home when meeting with legislators and the press. "[Other gay rights groups] used to walk around the building and they would tell people, 'Bring in your wedding photos.' And we would tell people, 'Don't bring in your wedding photos, whatever you do!' . . . They [members of the public] can deal with us having long-term committed relationships. They can deal with us needing benefits and protections. But the two wedding dresses, its ick. Two guys in tuxedos, ick."

Underlying these activist framing strategies—packaging marriage either as rights and security or as love and commitment—was a need for activists to tell their stories in ways that would serve the imperatives of a commercial news media system and appeal to mainstream audiences. Certainly the strategy on the part of gay rights activists to present homosexuality as normal and banal is not unique to the marriage debate. As Barry Adam (2003) has pointed out, these same universalizing discourses ran throughout the gays-in-the-military debate throughout the 1990s. "Gay and lesbian organizations attempted to place military men and women before the cameras . . . by showing their ordinariness and, in some cases, their extraordinary service duly rewarded with medals and honor—but to no avail. They found themselves unable to disrupt the symbolic value that homosexuality-as-transgression holds in dominant masculinist and nationalist discourses and unable to place on the public agenda the mundane experiences of lesbian and gay people who have served in the military" (p. 267).

As Adam asserts, activist organizations' media strategies for reaching mainstream audiences are not always or often successful. In the following chapters, I explore these tensions by analyzing prominent print and broadcast news stories, along with activist critiques, in order to investigate how the marriage issue was characterized and symbolized by mainstream news outlets. This analysis uncovers how professional journalistic norms limited the debate to a two-sided conflict, revealing the hurdles that social movement actors face when attempting to shape a controversial issue on the national media stage.

Conclusion: Wedded to the Marriage Issue, for Better and for Worse

As the dust settled after the 2004 presidential election, the gay rights movement began repairing the damage from what the national media referred to as a series of "bruising losses" (Broder, 2004, p. 1). President George W. Bush was reelected, running a successful campaign that won the "values vote," including a proposed constitutional ban on gay marriage. By large majorities, citizens of 11 states voted to pass state constitutional amendments prohibiting same-sex marriages. Making matters worse, several gay ally groups on the political left blamed the gay marriage issue for President Bush's reelection. At first it appeared that the battle over same-sex-marriage rights, rather than winning gay and lesbian citizens the legitimacy they had been fighting for, may have cost them quite a bit. As many in the movement had initially feared, the marriage issue had produced a vehement backlash, the kind social movements struggle to recover from. In those "dark days," one pessimistic editorial opined, the best strategy was for gay and lesbian advocates to "hunker down," as if hibernating like a bear for a long winter. "Over the next four years, the GLBT community isn't going to have much to cheer about: no federal civil rights legislation, no federal hate crimes laws, paltry increases in AIDS funding, and, of course, a continual verbal onslaught against us by our elected officials. It's going to be a hard, cold freeze."

Perhaps the question of gay marriage, cloaked in an overall concern for equality for gay and lesbian citizens, was placed on the ballot a little too early for the vast majority of the American public. As the communications special-ist for the Human Rights Campaign put it, "On Election Day the American people were given the final exam on the first day of class." The marriage conversation, as we saw unfold over the next several years, was only in the beginning stages of what would be a very long discussion.

These considerable losses in the aftermath of the 2004 election left the gay rights movement struggling to put the pieces back together again. News coverage reported that the larger national organizations like the HRC were pursuing "less aggressive" strategies, appointing non-gay leaders, and bolster-ing their memberships of straight allies. Several groups backed away from the marriage issue in lieu of pursuing less controversial equality measures, such as social security survivor benefits, hospital visitation, and tax breaks for same-sex families.

As this chapter has shown, for most of my informants, gay marriage may not have the platform of choice to lobby for increased equality and antidis-crimination measures. The onslaught of media attention forced marriage to become the central issue of the movement, pushing gay rights activists into a bitter and increasingly public battle against many of society's most power-ful political forces. But the debate did pave the way for several simultaneous transformations. It increased the visibility of a number of LGBT concerns, provided a space for new, "reformed" images of the community, and boosted mobilization efforts of the gay rights movement.

For all of the groups I spoke with, the marriage debate carried out in the press provided a rallying point, elevating the status of their community and their issues. In some cases the issue even contributed to the growth of their organization either in terms of donations, members, litigation efforts, or political interest. In others the press attention over marriage forced a differ-ent conversation altogether. For example, leaders of the small, state-based group Indiana Equality, immersed in a conservative political environment, feared that the national press attention surrounding marriage might ham-per their attempts to pass moderate measures at the state level. At the time, Indiana Equality was working on amending the state's civil rights code to include gender orientation and sexual identity orientation as part of its an-tidiscrimination policies. But when same-sex nuptials began in other parts of the country in 2004, leaders of the organization knew gay marriage would become a battle at the state level, and a losing one at that. Leaders had to shift organizational resources to fight a state amendment banning same-sex marriages. Not surprisingly, gay rights advocates lost. Nevertheless, the battle itself provided a point of mobilization, an opportunity to gain new members and motivate constituents at the grassroots level. As their PR director told me, in losing the marriage battle at the state level, "at the same time we've also used [the marriage debate] as an organizing tool to get more people here engaged [in activism] across the state."

At the same time, the marriage issue also pushed activists to produce and employ discourses that soften and normalize gay identity for straight audiences rather than embarking on a more radical and systematic critique of embedded cultural homophobia. These activist informants, ever aware of the power of media images and understandably cautious of offending mainstream sensibilities, strove to tap into universalizing stories and pictures to represent their cause and their community. Other groups in the movement—the voices from within the gay community who argue that marriage may not be worth the fight—were shut out of this debate. With an overall concern for making gay and lesbian life palatable for a mainstream audience, the marriage equality movement arguably "narrow[ed] its political horizons and temper[ed] its actions to avoid hostilities with heterosexist (and intermittently homophobic) mass media" (Carroll & Ratner, 1999, p. 20).

The diversity that has been so central to the gay movement has kept competing political logics—those oppositional and assimilationist discourses discussed at the beginning of this chapter—in equilibrium. Gay movement scholars have argued that, historically, "The peculiar brilliance of the gay identity movement has been due to the way identity, interest group and commercialism have been held in balance . . . The movement grew in many directions at the same time, but without having a center. It was not forced to homogenize around a narrow vision of goals, identities and strategy" (Armstrong, 2002, p. 189).

This is certainly not to argue that the more progressive arms of the movement representing queer politics have disappeared altogether. Nor does it discount the opportunities that the marriage conversation affords the larger LGBT community, a subject I return to in the concluding chapter. Nevertheless, as marriage equality comes to dominate the movement's agenda and become the stand-in issue for inclusive citizenship, gay and lesbian identity risks becoming homogenized and diluted. As Armstrong (2002) warns, while "the decentralized and expressive nature of the movement allowed space for diverse ways of being gay," in the move toward "ideological homogenization, these spaces may disappear" (p. 189). For a movement that has thrived on its diversity, exclusive emphasis on marriage could force gay and lesbian identity into a rigid box from which it cannot easily escape.

3. "The Marrying Kind"

The Face of Gay Marriage in the News

The July 7, 2003, edition of *Newsweek* magazine featured two "poster couples"—one gay and one lesbian—to symbolize the controversial, captivating, and soon-to-be pervasive issue of gay marriage. *Newsweek*'s cover director, Bruce Ramsay, decided to do a "split run" for that week, producing alternate covers of the same magazine issue (White, 2003). One *Newsweek* cover photo featured a medium shot of two young Caucasian women, smiling warmly, both facing the camera. One woman stands behind the other and cradles her in an embrace, their hands clasped at their hips. The couple, who could easily be mistaken for sisters and possibly even twins, is dressed nearly identically: both wear dark, fitted denim jeans and crisp white shirts. Their faces, which touch lightly at their foreheads, feature similar makeup—modern and professional, fresh and light. They appear to be in their early 30s and do not violate the traditional cover girl standards of beauty, thinness, or youth. Their styling, posture, obvious makeup and jewelry, and manicured nails mark the women as appropriately feminine. Nothing about the cover, even the somewhat intimate posture they hold, is especially threatening, except for the headline inscribed in large bold type across their torsos: "Is gay marriage next?"

The alternate *Newsweek* cover for that same week features a gay male couple: two conventionally fit and attractive Caucasian men who appear to be in their 30s or early 40s. They are arranged similarly, one man with his arms draped around the other, their hands clasped at the waist. The pose is comparable in its banality to that of the lesbian couple, though the representation of *male* intimacy offers a potentially more threatening image for *Newsweek*'s largely heterosexual audience.

In a split-run cover story, the July 7, 2003, edition of *Newsweek* magazine featured two "poster couples"—one gay male and one lesbian couple—to symbolize the controversial issue of same-sex marriage. The cover story was not centrally about gay marriage, but about the impact of the landmark U.S. Supreme Court case, *Lawrence v. Texas*. (From *Newsweek*, July 2 © 2003 The Newsweek/Daily Beast Company LLC. All rights reserved. Used by permission and protected by the Copyright Laws of the United States. The printing, copying, redistribution, or retransmission of the material without express written permission is prohibited.)

These prominent magazine covers during the summer of 2003—months before the historic *Goodridge* case, months before the mayor of San Francisco began handing out marriage licenses to same-sex couples—mark the beginning of the contemporary debate over same-sex-marriage rights in the mainstream press. Nevertheless, despite what the headline implies, *Newsweek*'s cover story that week was not about gay marriage per se, but about the historic U.S. Supreme Court case handed down on the final day of the Court's 2002–2003 term, *Lawrence v. Texas*. In a 6–3 decision, the Supreme Court overturned the Texas anti-sodomy law, citing that gays and lesbians "are entitled to respect for their private lives" (E. Thomas, 2003, p. 40). The decision was hailed as one of the most important opinions of the last century, on par with *Roe v. Wade* and *Brown v. Board of Education*. The *Lawrence* case also led the mainstream media, along with politicians, legal scholars, social conservatives, and gay rights activists, to focus public attention on same-sex-marriage rights. Although the majority opinion was careful in arguing that the case was not about gay marriage, conservative justice Antonin Scalia quipped, "Do not believe it" (E. Thomas, 2003, p. 42).

This cover story on "gay marriage" was not really about gay marriage, and it was also not especially clear why these two couples were selected by *Newsweek* to represent the movement. The couples were not linked to either the *Lawrence* or the *Goodridge* cases nor any other sort of legislative effort to legalize gay marriage. They were not identified as activists in the movement for marriage equality. Though *visually* very prominent, the cover couples selected are noticeably absent from the newsmagazine's textual content. Their stories and images do not appear in the inside pages of the spread. Reading the brief inside note from the editor, all that readers are told is that Dominic and Andrew had a civil union ceremony in Vermont and are raising twins in New York; Lauren and Noel are engaged and planning a commitment ceremony later in the spring. But their presence on the *Newsweek* covers exemplifies a pattern in terms of how gay and lesbian couples appeared in the news: as visual ornaments. At closer look their selection reveals a larger systematic effort that projected the face of gay marriage in predictable ways: one that was overwhelmingly white, middle to upper class, and anchored to dominant notions of masculinity and femininity.

This chapter is centered on representations of gay and lesbian couples, their ceremonies, and their families in news narratives. Analyzing prominent national news coverage from a range of print and broadcast media from 2003 through 2005,[1] I examine the extent to which activists were able to assert their preferred images and narratives in news discourse. This time period is significant not only because of the *intense* media saturation of the issue but also because this was the timeframe in which journalists *first* began to describe, assess, symbolize and frame the issue. In chapters 5 and 6 I show how visual representations and framing of the issue evolved from this initial time period to the later coverage in 2008 through 2010.

This chapter highlights how gay life was no longer "othered" in stereotypical ways, but, as my activist informants desired, was shown conforming to normative and disciplined definitions of marriage and family. These "poster couples" selected by news producers and gay rights activists were frequently legitimated in news narratives, but often unwittingly at the expense of the broader community of unmarried gays, who were relegated to the margins.

To begin I examine the linguistic and visual devices that news entities relied upon to represent gay and lesbian couples as "deserving" of marriage. What were the characteristics of the gay and lesbian couples who were selected to represent the marriage movement? What kinds of images of gay and lesbian life did the news media foreground? What were the predominant narratives that gay and lesbian couples who were given a voice in the news used to talk about and define their marriage? Building on the work of critical-cultural and queer theorists, my analysis in this chapter focuses on how markers of gender, class, race, lifestyle, and sexuality were deployed to construct the human face of gay marriage.

In the second part of the chapter, I move from the couples to their wedding ceremonies, specifically the ways in which same-sex weddings were ritualized and symbolized in news narratives. How were standard ceremonial symbols (rings, cakes, flowers) and dress (wedding gowns and tuxedos) used to represent same-sex ceremonies in the news? In what ways were these symbols used to reinforce heterosexual binaries (e.g., man/woman, bride/groom)? Finally, I conclude this chapter by considering how these stories and images work together to produce new forms of gay desire.

The Importance of Being Seen: Visual Discourses in News Narratives

Visuals serve as important editorial content that are able to frame issues in powerful ways that words cannot (Messaris & Abraham, 2001). My focus on representations, in both the visual and verbal form, is a critical component in understanding how news narratives were used to tell the story of gay marriage. Moreover, recent scholarship suggests that visual discourses are often excluded in news analysis. For example, while the combined audience share for television news is great, some mass communication scholars have argued that TV news is under-studied (Bucy & Grabe, 2007; Grabe, 2007; Grabe & Bucy, 2009). When television news is the subject of analysis, the visual content of news narration is often excluded at the expense of privileging verbal content (e.g., a focus on transcripts rather than video). While visuals are very much produced and constructed—as much as the written or spoken word—"images are readily accepted as closely resembling what they represent in the physical world. Therefore viewers are less likely to question their constructedness" (Grabe, 2007, p. 7). Despite the importance of visual and verbal narratives in news discourse, most critical work has had a heavy *textual* emphasis that rarely includes an analysis of images and how they work together to produce narratives of gay and lesbian life (Landau, 2009).

Despite the lack of scholarship on visual news narratives, the *perceived* visual impact of gay marriage imagery was touted early on by conservative activists and political analysts as having a "rallying" effect that stirred the conservative base into action. As conservative activist Randy Thomasson expressed in a *60 Minutes* (March 10, 2004) interview:

> BOB SIMON (JOURNALIST): What went through your mind when you first saw those television pictures of gays lined up at city hall waiting to get married?
> RANDY THOMASSON (EXECUTIVE DIRECTOR OF THE CAMPAIGN FOR CALIFORNIA FAMILIES): I think I was as shocked as most people were, because this was now out of the closet and *all over the TV screen*. And then night after night, day after day, it was in your face. And this was not just shocking, this angered and actually disgusted a lot of parents and grandparents who didn't want that being pushed into their living room every day [emphasis added].

Likewise, the political director of ABC News compared the visual potency of gay and lesbian wedding ceremonies to the images that exposed the Abu Ghraib prison scandal: "We saw in those prison abuse photos out of Iraq, . . . the country's attention can really be focused by photographs, by moving images. People on both sides of this [gay marriage] issue are going to watch to see how much the activists get engaged by the photos, by the pictures" (Kennedy, 2004).

Through my analysis of media content, then, I was interested in the process by which a group that has historically symbolized the "antithesis" of wholesome family values and the opposite of monogamous partnering comes to represent lifelong commitment and enduring family life. This move, of course, is a tenuous one, predicated on the adherence of these select "poster couples" to conventional heteronormative logics. As I highlight in chapter 1, being seen is not the same thing as being known (Walters, 2001a). A growing line of critical-cultural scholarship has shown how gay and lesbian representation has operated within specific heterosexist power structures that demand imposed conformity to a perceived heterosexual audience, leaving dominant ideologies firmly intact (see chapter 1 for a discussion, as well as Dow, 2001; Fejes, 2000; Gross, 2001; Walters, 2001a, 2001b).

Likewise, I argue in this chapter that the couples who appeared in national news stories about gay marriage were selected to appeal to a presumed typical news audience—heterosexual, middle to upper class, and educated. Through the language and imagery used, news audiences and readers were continuously reassured that these couples and their unions were "traditional," "normal," "ordinary," not "scary," and not any more "interesting" than a typical heterosexual couple. Moreover, these married couples and their lifestyles, presented as suburban, wholesome, and average, were oftentimes marked as different from and more acceptable than the rest of the LGBT community, cast as urban, alternative, and deviant.

In order to critically analyze the "discursive politics" embedded in emerging news narratives during this time period, I employed both in-depth, qualitative textual analysis and systematic quantitative content analysis. I began by exploring those news "packages" that were intended to give readers and viewers more "complete," "in-depth" coverage of the issue: prominent and lengthy feature articles and cover stories. I searched the Lexis-Nexis database to locate front-page features in national newspapers, cover stories in leading national newsmagazines, and leading prime-time newscasts in which the entire episode was exclusively focused on the gay marriage issue (see the appendix for selection criteria and a list of news stories). Approximately 25 stories were selected, including feature or cover stories from national newsmagazines *Time, Newsweek,* and *U.S. News & World Report*; prominent front-page stories from leading national newspapers like the *New York Times* and the *Washington Post*; and episodes of prime-time television news programs *60 Minutes, 20/20,* and *Nightline.* These programs and publications were selected because of their prominence and their appeal to large, mainstream news audiences. I had a particular interest in televised "newsmagazines" like *60 Minutes* and *Nightline* because of their "self-contained narrative segments [that] allow for elaborate storytelling" and rich visual narration (Grabe, 2000, p. 40).

The results from the textual analysis were then used to systematically "test" for patterns across a wider range of television network news stories. Through critical analysis of these patterns, content analysis provides a powerful tool for researchers to investigate the "big ideas" that shape cultural meanings, "the contours of the ideological environment" (S. Thomas, 1994, p. 689). I used content analysis to investigate 93 television news stories that were centrally concerned about the gay marriage issue that aired on NBC, CBS, and *ABC* evening newscasts between June 2003 and January 2005. Content analysis was used to systematically capture the ways in which broadcast news entities framed the issue of same-sex marriage, privileged particular sources over others, and depicted gay and lesbian couples and their ceremonies. This chapter reports on the findings of the qualitative content analysis and how these patterns emerged through quantitative content analysis.

Seen But Not Heard: Nameless, Voiceless Couples Symbolize the Movement

As chapter 2 highlights, activists fully realized that the unprecedented amount of reporting on the issue of same-sex marriage presented an opportunity for gays and lesbians to appear in ways they hadn't been able to before: not as criminals, victims, or radicals, but as newlyweds and families. They were also acutely aware of the power of visual framing—that the visuals carried into the living rooms of Americans by mainstream news outlets, and in particular full-motion video of same-sex couples kissing, exchanging rings, and cheering in celebration, would shape public perceptions of the community and the marriage issue.

Media analysis during this time period revealed an interesting pattern: in most stories, gays and lesbians were presented as unidentified couples who were either standing in line waiting for a marriage license or celebrating during their ceremony. We as viewers and readers do not meet them; we do not know their names, where they are from, how they met, or why they want to get married. These couples are not given a voice; they do not speak and are not quoted. In print they largely appear in photographs but are not cited in the article or named in the caption. In fact, content analysis of television news reports during this same time period showed that when gay and lesbian couples were visually featured in a story, their names were revealed only 18.4 percent of the time, either through the reporter's narration or as text appearing across the screen.

This figure is shockingly low considering that attribution of sources is a standard journalistic practice. Attributing names to the sources used in news reports not only increases the credibility and power of the source interviewed but also helps viewers identify with the speaker. Historically, however, the question of anonymity has been a contentious issue in reporting on gay and lesbian communities. For decades, news organizations "protected" the anonymity of their gay sources by assigning them pseudonyms and hiding or blurring their images. This standard practice of masking the identity of gay and lesbian sources was often necessary, since gays and lesbians feared losing their jobs or

SAN FRANCISCO, CA: News stories regularly featured long lines of gay and
lesbian couples wrapped around city blocks, as in this photograph taken outside of
San Francisco City Hall on February 19, 2004. On August 12, 2004, the California
Supreme Court voided the marriages of about 4,000 gay couples performed by the
city of San Francisco, ruling that the mayor had overstepped his authority. (Photo
by Hector Mata/AFP/Getty Images)

being ostracized by their community. (This fear still legitimately exists, since
in 34 states one can be fired for being gay or lesbian; in 44 states one can be
fired for being transgender.) In any case, the refusal of editors, reporters, and
perhaps even the couples themselves to be identified in the vast majority of
news stories appears contrary to journalistic norms. In addition, the anonymity
contradicts the seemingly very public *visual* exposure of their marriage and
family to national news audiences (Landau, 2009, p. 87). This treatment most
likely has less to do with privacy concerns and more to do with how couples
were used in stories, as background b-roll in almost a "zoo people" fashion, as
objects on display rather than as the substantive subject of a news report.

As previously indicated, gays and lesbians were certainly not absent from
news reports on gay marriage. On the contrary, systematic content analysis
of network news during this time period showcased how gay and lesbian
people were visually resonant in same-sex-marriage coverage, appearing in
92.5 percent of the stories. However, while these couples were visually resonant, they remained mostly silent, their voices and perspectives not heard.
In fact, of the 244 couples who appeared in broadcast news stories (as the
central feature of a shot), only 20.5 percent were given the opportunity to

speak at all. Even those select few who were cited spent the majority of their on-air time in silent b-roll (on average 23 seconds) as opposed to speaking (9 seconds).

This discrepancy between the speaking and non-speaking roles (Roberts, 1975) of marginalized groups in news coverage is not unique to the coverage of gay civil rights issues. Previous research has shown how historically marginalized communities are often visually present in television news stories even when they are not granted the power to speak. For example, television news coverage of the black community may afford African Americans a great deal of visual prominence, often in the form of a mug shot or video of a suspect being handcuffed or restrained by a police officer. However, rarely are they given the opportunity to speak or offer their own interpretation of events (Entman, 1992; Owens, 2008; Poindexter, Smith & Heider, 2003). More than 30 years ago, Roberts (1975) identified this discrepancy between the speaking and non-speaking news appearances of people of color and concluded that although African-Americans could be seen in television news stories, they were rarely heard. Problematically, we might "expect" this discrepancy to be evident in coverage in which gays are criminalized and victimized (e.g., stories about bath houses, coverage of AIDS, etc.); however, the relative silence of gay and lesbian citizens continues even in the reporting of gay civil rights issues (Barnhurst 2003; Liebler et al., 2009).

This pattern persists in newsmagazine reporting as well. Early coverage presented images of gay and lesbian couples, or crowds of protesters, without identifying them or citing them as sources in the story. The August 25, 2003, edition of *U.S. News & World Report*, headlined "Gays Force the Issue," featured a crowd of unidentified, presumably gay, lesbian and allied people clapping and embracing in celebration of the Supreme Court's overturn of Texas anti-sodomy laws (Gilgoff, 2003). Similarly, in a later edition, *U.S. News & World Report* prominently features a gay male couple and, further in the magazine spread, a lesbian couple holding their toddler son during what appears to be their wedding ceremonies. Neither couple is named, cited, or identified; instead the caption reads vaguely and anonymously, "They do. Thousands of same-sex couples are getting married in San Francisco" (Gilgoff, 2004). The close-up shot of longtime activists Molly McKay and Davina Kotulski in *Newsweek* does not identify the activists by name, but instead writes, "In California, a couple marks a win." Likewise, the February 24, 2004, issue of *Newsweek* featured a photograph of Del Martin and Phyllis Lyon, an activist couple who had been together since the 1950s and were married in June 2008. The caption does not identify the couple, explain the significance of the women, or cite them in the story, but rather reads, "A marriage in San Francisco" (Breslau, 2004).

Generally speaking, then, this analysis has shown that the marriage equality movement was represented by hundreds of nameless, sometimes faceless, and often voiceless gay and lesbian couples who appeared in long lines wrapped around city blocks waiting to obtain marriage licenses. As chapter 2 indicated, these were hardly the kinds of images gay marriage advocates preferred. Most gay activists feared that "straight" news audiences would disconnect from images of masses of couples, looking more like a "rock concert" or "Mardi Gras" than a wedding, and sought to foreground stories of individual couples and their private ceremonies.

Alternately, in some news photographs individual couples were featured embracing during their ceremony, surrounded by supportive onlookers, but were not named, identified, or cited in the story. Despite the overall anonymity and relative silence of couples in the news—in particular "in-depth," lengthier news segments—news producers "introduced" audiences to a gay or lesbian couple or family. Newspaper reports, too, were much more likely to include the names of couples featured in photographs and cite them in the stories themselves. When gay and lesbian couples were featured, not just as visual ornaments but as the central focus of a news story, it provided the opportunity to interrogate the verbal and visual discursive strategies employed to normalize same-sex relationships and families.

The "Untraditional" Traditional Family: Mainstreaming Gay Marriage

While most same-sex couples who emerged in the mainstream news remained unidentified, some feature stories focused on a couple's meeting, falling in love, eventual decision to marry, and their marriage ceremony. When gay couples were prominently featured in these kinds of stories, they had to meet certain prerequisites. These poster couples weren't considered scary or threatening, audiences were assured, so long as they subscribed to conventional ideological norms and often heterosexist notions of partnering, monogamy, marriage, family, and parenting.

Overwhelmingly, when print and broadcast newsmagazines introduced audiences to gay marrieds in this time period, the pair was almost always an older Caucasian lesbian couple in their 50s or 60s who had been together for anywhere from 15 to 25 years. We meet them in their homes, usually in their kitchen (the culturally inscribed domestic space), surrounded by their children and family members. When they are not being interviewed, the b-roll footage includes them engaged in "normal" mundane domestic activities: preparing meals, eating and talking at the dinner table, and walking the dog around the block.

For example, the *60 Minutes* episode that aired on March 10, 2004, titled "Marry Me!" (Hewitt, 2004) goes to great lengths to present the face of gay marriage as one that is palatable to a mainstream heteronormative audience, being careful to set this couple of choice apart from gays and lesbians who live out their "alternative lifestyles." About eight minutes into the *60 Minutes* investigation on the issue of gay marriage, we meet Carol and Kay, an English teacher and a poet, who appear to be in their late 50s or early 60s. Reporter Bob Simon tells us that the couple has been together 25 years. Viewers hear their emotional story about waiting in the rain in a long line to obtain a marriage license. As they talk, a still photo of their ceremony appears on the screen; it simply shows the couple facing each other, holding hands. News producers juxtapose the image of Carol and Kay with a black-and-white still photograph of another couple married at San Francisco's city hall: Marilyn Monroe and Joe DiMaggio. As the photo of Monroe and DiMaggio cues the viewer to the dysfunctional, drugged-out, and all-too-short marriage of the famous Hollywood couple, the audience is assured that "Carol and Kay's marriage will last longer" than that of their heterosexual counterpart. As the reporter narrates the story of their ceremony, b-roll images show Carol and Kay preparing a meal, sitting at the kitchen table with their family, and showing their grandchildren a slide show of their wedding on the computer.

In stark contrast to the storyline of Carol and Kay, news producers create a juxtaposition of images to show how the couple's suburban family life is markedly different from stereotypical depictions of "gay life"—wild, sexually explicit, urban, youthful, alternative, and transgressive. Leaving suburbia, news crews transport the audience to the Castro, a famously gay neighborhood in San Francisco, often thought of as the capital of the gay liberation movement. The camera pans several faceless, anonymous couples, predominantly male, their backs to us, the camera focusing only on their lower torsos as they hold hands. We see medium-length shots of men in stereotypically gay urban wear—fitted jeans; too-tight, shrunken, ripped T-shirts; and leather jackets. Bob Simon's voiceover tells viewers: "You can't do a story on gays in San Francisco without visiting the Castro, the city's overwhelmingly gay neighborhood. Not every gay person in the Castro was ready to take the plunge into marriage; many preferred their alternative lifestyles. But most said they were ready to fight for the right to marry."

In another rupture, news audiences are presented with the b-roll footage of what appears to be a gay pride parade of a bygone era—though we're not told what year, or even what decade, it is taking place. The camera focuses in on a close-up shot of hands clapping and a crowd of people cheering against a background of colorful balloons and rainbow flags. In the next shot, drag queens with exposed body and facial hair, dressed in spaghetti-strap lingerie with lace, colorful boas draped around their necks, and long hair. They take on a performative stance toward the camera as they dance down the middle of the street. A prominent banner reads "Proud Strong United," followed by a group of protesters marching through the streets holding rainbow flags, cheering, and chanting. The audio that accompanies these images is loud and pronounced, filled with music, clapping, shouting, and street noises. Reporter Bob Simon's voice-over invokes stereotypes of gay promiscuity as he tells audiences, "A few decades ago, marriage was as far from the minds of gays as celibacy. Hardly a person in this parade gave it a thought."

After this brief visit to the urban center of the Castro, the camera returns us to the suburbs—as Simon says, back to "the home of Carol and Kay and their untraditional, traditional family." Sitting across from the two women, he says, "The fact is that today polls show that most Americans do not believe in gay marriage; they believe that marriage should be between a man and a woman. What can the two of you say to convince these Americans . . . ?" He is interrupted by Kay, who employs universalizing discourses to convince audiences that their relationship is nothing different from anyone else's: "Simply more exposure to faces like ours, ordinary lives like ours. Seeing this—seeing this on television in their own home, and seeing that we just flat don't look scary and that we're really not more interesting than they are will make the difference and should make the difference." The segment ends with Carol inviting TV viewers to just come by for dinner, in an apparent attempt to have viewers witness for themselves how normal and nonthreatening their family is.

These same discourses stand out in another prime-time news program: the February 24, 2004, *Nightline* episode that visits couples in order to find out "what exactly has changed" since the state of Massachusetts legalized same-sex marriages (Sievers, 2004, February 24). Both poster couples featured in the segment—Dave Wilson and Rob Compton, and Hillary and Julie Goodridge—were plaintiffs in the *Goodridge* case. They are interviewed in their home, in their kitchen and at their dining room table, symbols of the home's domesticity. B-roll of the couples preparing meals—warming spaghetti sauce and boiling water—also serve as markers of class. Both couples boast modern, stylish, contemporary kitchens with stainless steel appliances, granite countertops, and recessed lighting.

Their representations and talk of marriage speak to the discursive strategies that gay and lesbian couples relied on to define the institution of marriage, either as a package of rights or as the ultimate expression of love and commitment. As chapter 2 demonstrates, these definitional strategies represented a core divide within the movement. Those who wanted to talk about equality, reflecting a civil rights discourse, felt that love language was distracting, beside the point, and a harder pill for perceived straight audiences to swallow (as, the logic goes, straights do not like to envision or acknowledge same-sex love). Those who wanted to talk about marriage as love felt that it was a more universal approach (not too many hetero couples say they want to marry for the tax benefits, for example) and that majorities are often turned off by talk of minority rights—what they often see as "special rights."

The first couple featured, Dave Wilson and Rob Compton, appeared in several news texts to narrate their story of how they met and to describe what their life together is like. In this *Nightline* episode, Wilson and Compton, a mixed-race couple, shared with news audiences images and video from their ceremony.[2] Like most couples in the news, they said their original motivation was to acquire the same rights and benefits afforded to heterosexual couples. During the interview, Dave and Rob speak mostly of their marriage in terms of the legal rights and benefits, using terms like "rights," "security," "safety," and "next of kin." They explain that their desire to marry came about when Rob was in the hospital a few years back with kidney stones, and Dave was appalled that he had no say in any of Rob's medical decisions.

BOSTON, MA: David Wilson (top right) and Robert Compton (top left) speak to the media after being married by a Unitarian minister at the Arlington Street Church in Boston on May 17, 2004. Wilson and Compton, one of the first couples in Massachusetts to be legally wed, regularly appeared in news features about the gay marriage issue. (Photo by Stan Honda/AFP/Getty Images)

But beyond discourses of legal rights and benefits, Dave tells the story of their wedding, and talks emotionally about the weightiness of the moment in their ceremony when the officiate married them, saying, "and with the power vested in me." The power of that moment overwhelmed them, and, as Dave told *Nightline,* "we just became mush." Invoking the universality of marriage, Dave discussed the "intangible benefits" of being married, how they are now part of an institution that has uniform meaning: "We don't have to explain who we are or what we are to each other." Dave's rhetoric invokes a mainstreaming of same-sex romance as "love," a universal humanizing language that needs no explanation.

Likewise, the Goodridges, who were interviewed in the same *Nightline* segment, talk about their marriage as an amazing and historic event; while they knew of the legal benefits, they did not anticipate how much it would solidify their relationship and lend credibility to their family. They talked about their marriage through the eyes of their eight-year-old daughter, Annie. She was the catalyst for the historic case that bears their name legalizing same-sex marriage in Massachusetts. In a story they retold across news media, including *Nightline* and *Newsweek,* it was three years ago when Annie told her parents that they can't possibly love each other, because they were not married like the parents of other kids at her school. They discuss what their marriage meant to Annie in terms of a heteronormative sameness to her peers. "For her, it means that her family is like the other kids' families ... The level of both relief and, I think, comfort and security she feels has really been visible since May 17."

Seemingly curious about the emotional weight the couple placed on their marriage, the reporter pushes them by saying, "When you went into this, the legal rights, at least when I spoke to you before, seemed to be paramount." They both confirm, that, yes, that was originally all they were looking for. "But what we got in addition to that is a recognition and a sense of profound respect and love by the community that we weren't counting on before."

These couples cited in the news welcome a new era when gays and lesbians—at least the married ones—do not have to explain their relationship to their family, peers, schools, or community. Marriage, for them, ensures full integration and inclusive citizenship. But as critics like Suzanna Walters (2001b) and Michael Warner (1999) argue, "The-battle-has-been-won" discourse can be dangerous. Marriage is presented as the end-all, be-all goal for the gay and lesbian community, symbolizing full recognition by society, a sentiment shared by many of the activists I interviewed.

The notion that marriage equality is symbolic of full equality is echoed not only by gay and lesbian spokespeople cited in the news but also by reporters themselves. In news coverage the larger LGBT movement is reduced to a

BOSTON, MA: Hillary Goodridge (second from left); Julie Goodridge (right); their daughter, Annie (second from right); and lawyer Mary Bonauto (far left) of the Gay and Lesbian Advocates and Defenders (GLAD) celebrate as they leave city hall in Boston. On May 17, 2004, the Goodridges became the first same-sex couple in the city to be allowed to apply for a marriage license. Bonauto was the lead lawyer in the case that legalized gay marriage in Massachusetts, and the Goodridges were the lead couple of a total of 14 plaintiffs in the case. (Photo by Stan Honda/AFP/Getty Images)

single-issue movement (marriage), with little to no recognition of the inter-community conflicts over the marriage issue. As Ted Koppel tells audiences, "Make no mistake about it, gay marriage is an American revolution in the making" (Sievers, 2004, February 24). The *New York Times* coverage of the Massachusetts weddings reports that the newly marrieds "are acutely aware of their role as representatives of a new era for gays and lesbians" (Belluck, 2004b, p. A1). This type of journalistic narration presumes that gaining marriage rights (in what was, at the time, one state) erases the prejudice and inequality gays and lesbians have historically endured—and continue to endure—when it comes to accessing health-care, housing, employment, and hate crimes protections.

Just as the selection of gay and lesbian couples is anchored to heteronorma-tive notions of marriage, so too are the ways in which same-sex ceremonies are portrayed. Now that I have analyzed the selection of couples granted a presence and given a voice, I turn to how same-sex ceremonies have been ritualized and symbolized in news narratives.

BOSTON, MA: Hillary (left) and Julie Goodridge (right) display their rings after their marriage ceremony at the Unitarian Universalist Association on May 17, 2004, in Boston. As the lead plaintiff couple in the court case that legalized gay marriage in Massachusetts, the couple and their family were regularly featured in news stories. (Photo by Stan Honda/AFP/Getty Images)

With This Ring: Symbolizing and Ritualizing Same-Sex Ceremonies

While same-sex marriage ceremonies presented in the news and popular culture offer the opportunity to show unique, alternative versions that might be more applicable to gay and lesbian couples—a possible "queering" of traditional marriage—the result is often to "depict gay weddings as cheerfully hetero we-are-the-world assimilation" (Walters, 2001b, p. 341).

The gay and lesbian ceremonies featured in news stories, through imagery and descriptive text, do more to mimic dominant media representations of the heterosexist institution than to question or challenge it. These sentimental representations of the wedding ceremony—either heterosexual or homosexual—ultimately serve the commercial interests of a number of institutions tied closely to the wedding industry, including the diamond, fashion, floral, and culinary industries, to name a few. Ultimately these consumerist representations have come to define the modern wedding ceremony for same-sex couples as well, undoubtedly in an attempt to tap into the perceived budding market of the gay consumer.

Oftentimes these news productions of same-sex ceremonies constrained representations of gay weddings and forced couples into heterosexual binaries, simply inserting into traditional wedding symbols and imagery two women or two men. News organizations created and selected graphics that strongly mimicked heterosexual pairings to represent the issue of gay marriage. One of the most common and consistent graphics used was a reconfiguration of the iconic miniature bride-and-groom figurine often featured as a cake topper on towering white wedding cakes. For example, the predominant graphic that *Nightline* used to open its February 24, 2004, newscast was of a spinning wedding cake topped with alternating figurines—one cake with a mixed-sex couple figurine, one cake with two bride figurines, and one cake with two groom figurines. These alternating images flashed between contrasting images of a lesbian couple kissing during their ceremony and a sound bite from President Bush calling for a constitutional amendment to ban gay marriage.

Likewise, the May 8, 2005, Sunday Styles section of the *New York Times* featured a front-page article on gay weddings, with almost the entire space above the fold featuring three dozen or so ceramic wedding figurines—women in wedding gowns, men in tuxedos—organized along same-sex pairings (Bellafante, 2005). The iconic figurine is even used in one *New York Times* article describing a couple's preparation for their big day: "On the windowsill above the sink, there was a figurine of two brides, and on their calendar was scrawled, simply, 'Get Married'" (Belluck, 2004b, p. A19). Indeed, the same-sex figurine was such a pervasive symbol that it was selected to represent the controversial *Newsweek* cover nearly five years later that covered the Prop 8 case in California. Two ceramic brides, gleaming white, stand out against a Pepto-Bismol-pink background with the divisive headline reading, "The conservative case for gay marriage."

In addition to cake toppers, other graphics produced by news organizations strongly reflect traditional opposite-sex wedding dress and rituals, now applied to same-sex pairings. For example, the *60 Minutes* episode titled "Marry Me!" (Hewitt, 2004, March 10) features a magazine-like close-up shot of two identical men, mirror images of each other, one angled forward facing the camera and the other one angled facing right. The two identical faces overlap each other in an intimate posture, appearing as if they are about to kiss. Below them, on the horizon, are a dozen or so photographically illustrated couples, brides in white gowns joined arm in arm with other brides, and grooms in tuxedos joined arm in arm with other grooms. The figures are dressed in traditional attire, the only difference from conventional wedding imagery being the same-sex pairings.

Interestingly, the graphical ways news organizations chose to represent the issue were rarely reflected in the actual footage and photographs of same-sex couples during their ceremonies. While it was fairly common to see two men dressed in tuxedos during their ceremony, it was rare to see two women pictured in traditional white wedding gowns. In the cases of real-life ceremonies that were predominantly featured, such as the wedding of Julie and Hillary Goodridge or the celebrity ceremony of Rosie and Kelly O'Donnell, the women were not wearing dresses at all, but light-colored pantsuits.

The symbol of the ring, perhaps the most iconic symbol of marriage and commitment, was a recurring image used in news stories. The lead photo—appearing in full color above the fold—on the front page of the *New York Times* the day after same-sex weddings began in Massachusetts, shows a gay male couple leaving the courthouse, one man prominently thrusting his ring finger in the air as if to show onlookers his wedding ring (Belluck, 2004a, p. A1). Both men smile widely as the city clerk who performed their ceremony gives the couple a thumbs-up. A close-up shot of the wedding ring or rings was also commonly used by television news crews to symbolically represent the issue. The February 24, 2004 *Nightline* episode that took us through the ceremonies and into the homes of two couples focused close-up shots on the ring-bearing hands of both Rob Compton and Dave Wilson and Julie and Hillary Goodridge. Additionally, photographs in newsmagazines were often positioned or angled to show rings on the hands of same-sex couples. For example, the July 7, 2003, *Newsweek* featured a medium-length shot of the hands of two men dressed in dark suits, one sliding a ring on his partner's hand (E. Thomas, 2003, p. 42).

The sameness to "traditional" wedding ceremonies and rituals was also emphasized in the series of articles leading up to "the big day" in Massachusetts when same-sex couples could legally marry. These articles emphasized the similarity of largely commercial wedding customs such as picking out wedding attire, shopping for rings, organizing reception details such as food and beverages, selecting flowers, and even going through the mental rituals of bridal jitters and cold feet.

The May 16, 2004, *New York Times* front page article with the headline "Hearts beat fast to opening strains of the gay-wedding march" chronicled how several couples and the city of Boston were preparing for the onslaught of gay nuptials (Belluck & Zezima, 2004). The article's most prominent photo is of a middle-age lesbian couple peering at each other over a glistening jewelry case, "shopping for their wedding rings," aided by a salesperson. Sprinkled

PROVINCETOWN, MA: Kristi Habedanck (left) and partner Suzanne Rotondo (right) of New York kiss as Rotondo holds the couple's daughter, Phoebe, after receiving their marriage license on May 17, 2004, in Provincetown, Massachusetts. (Photo by William B. Plowman/Getty Images)

among the reporting on how various opponents in the state have attempted to reverse the Massachusetts Supreme Court's decision on the legality of gay marriage, the article describes the "giddy anticipation," "anxious disbelief," and "exhilaration" of couples. The article goes on to report how "Linda Lundin and Kathy Bertrand, partners for 26 years, are planning their wedding attire: white linen pants and a pastel top for Ms. Lundin, a drapey peach-and-green pants outfit for Ms. Bertrand." When the Goodridges are interviewed in the same article, Julie narrates what is going through her mind: "I'm thinking about whether or not the shoes are going to look good with the suit I picked out . . . Is the tailor going to be done and have we ordered enough flowers and are we going to have fried calamari at the reception and how much is enough?" Explains one lesbian about to be married to her partner of 19 years, "I feel as emotionally invested as any bride. I have the bridal jitters."

Reports of the ceremonies performed that day contained the level of frivolous details that have been common in traditional newspaper reporting of heterosexual weddings. For example, one gay couple was described as marrying "on their 8 ½ acre Christmas tree farm in a stand of fading daffodils under an arch they had made from the ribs of a whale. The men wore lily-of-the-valley boutonnieres and stood behind a lilac bouquet as Mr. Bourn, a town selectman, read 'Oh Tell Me The Truth About Love' by W. H. Auden" (Belluck, 2004a, p. A21). Throughout these mundane reporting details, the similarity of a gay groom or a lesbian bride to any other heterosexual groom or bride is continuously emphasized.

When television news audiences were invited to witness in some detail a gay or lesbian couple's wedding ceremony, the propulsion to mimic customary heteronormative practices was even more pronounced. For example, when the July 13, 2004, *Nightline* episode opened on the wedding ceremony of Rob Compton and Dave Wilson, the setting was of a large, formal church with elaborate arches and architectural details, packed with hundreds of guests filling even the upper balcony of the church. The two men marched slowly down the aisle to traditional wedding music, played on the harp, both of them wearing black tuxedos. The ceremonial dress, setting, and music signified formality and tradition, with the exception of the rainbow flag hanging from the upper balcony of the church. In an emotional moment, the female officiate, clearly choking back tears, raised her hand to the couples and began reciting the ritualistic ceremonial words beginning "by the power vested in me," at which point the entire church erupted in applause and gave the couple a standing ovation.

Later on in the program, producers showed video clips of Julie and Hillary Goodridge's ceremony, which took place later that same afternoon. Both women wore white pantsuits and marched down the aisle of the church as guests sang a chorus of "Here Comes the Bride." While the full verse is inaudible in the *Nightline* episode, the *New York Times* reported that guests sang a revised version of the traditional wedding tune: "Here comes the brides, so gay with pride, isn't it a wonder that they somehow survived" (Belluck, 2004a, p. A21). Iconic wedding images reinforce the validity of their ceremony: the role of the flower girl is played by their eight-year-old daughter, Annie; cameras focus in on a close-up of their rings; and a traditional wedding kiss seals their union. In the representations of both of these ceremonies, audiences are assured that this is a wedding just like any other. Except for the fact that there are two brides or two grooms, these ceremonies do not offend the culturally constructed, taken-for-granted notions of what a wedding is or what one should look like. In the case of at least two of these selected media couples—the Goodridges and the O'Donnells—one partner took the last name of the other, ironically participating in a heterosexist and patriarchal practice historically rooted in property ownership.

Short of the Goodridges' revised lyrics to the wedding march, these featured ceremonies did not contain anything that resisted, questioned, or reimagined the institution of marriage, a deliberate strategy on the part of activists to select and highlight couples and ceremonies that did not challenge conventional notions of matrimony. (Recall Samiya's insistence that gay people are not "challenging" or "redefining" the institution of marriage.) In fact, the only aspect that marked these ceremonies as different from a traditional wedding was the prevalence of news cameras, both video and still, and the preponderance of reporters present. It was clear that these ceremonies served not merely as intimate pronunciations of love in front of friends and family but as organized media events as well. As I detail in the following chapter, these visual representations that constructed gay marriage as *symbolically similar to* heterosexual marriage contradicted news anchors' oral scripts of gay marriage being radically *different from* traditional marriage. It is this confrontation between sameness and difference that I return to in the book's concluding chapter.

Conclusion: Producing Marriage as Gay Desire

By deconstructing the visual and linguistic narratives used to tell the story of gay marriage in 2003 and 2004, this chapter has probed the central question, in this "era of the visible," in which depictions of gay and lesbian life appear with increased regularity, who and what is actually seen? This analysis has shown that, initially, only a select few were allowed entry into the conversation about marriage equality. News stories constructed these gay and lesbian "poster couples" as "normal": suburban, middle to upper class, Caucasian, nonthreatening in demeanor and appearance, anchored to appropriate depictions of femininity and masculinity, and already a part of a long-lasting, monogamous, child-rearing partnership. By scrutinizing the visual productions of same-sex wedding ceremonies, I highlighted how those who were selected by the media were careful not to question traditional cultural meanings of marriage or interrupt the symbolic imagery of wedding rituals.

Certainly, given the historic representations of the gay and lesbian community as promiscuous perverts and dangerous pedophiles, incapable of committed love and unfit for family life, *any* depiction that acknowledges same-sex ceremonies and features gay families represents progress, light-years ahead of the limited portrayals of gay life that propagated even a decade ago. Returning to Carol and Kay's call for "more exposure" to faces like theirs understandably reflects a powerful sentiment implying that increased visibility leads to greater societal acceptance. But in constructing the "ordinariness" of those gay and lesbian couples who are deemed worthy of marriage equality, news producers, through written narrative and selected imagery, also created dichotomies between those gays and lesbians who lead "normal" lives, similar to the perceived heterosexual news audience, and those more outlandish, sexually promiscuous homosexuals who live "alternative lifestyles" on the margins of society. In doing so, producers invoked a common discourse in the marriage debate, popular among gay conservatives as well, that marriage is the panacea that will "tame the wild beast" of gay culture and homosexual desire. As *60 Minutes* reporter Bob Simon told audiences, "Go to the Castro today, and the conversation has changed" (Hewitt, 2004, March 10). The video shots of banners and flags from the gay pride parade, icons of the gay liberation movement, faded to a final image of a lone rainbow flag blowing silently in the wind. The rainbow flag represents the historic residue of a bygone era rather than a symbol of modern activism.

We must therefore consider the ways in which these legitimating discourses also regulate gay identity (Landau, 2009, p. 88). In her analysis of same-sex parenting in mainstream U.S. newspapers and newsmagazines during this same time period, Landau concluded that these portrayals of gay family life only worked to reinforce heterosexist notions of partnering and parenting. Moreover, news texts focused almost exclusively on the *child* of a gay or lesbian couple—who was "compulsively" reinforced as heterosexual—as the "synecdoche and social test for gay familial life" (p. 82). Gay couples, in other words, were acceptable only if they reared straight, and appropriately masculine and feminine, children.

Likewise, the gay and lesbian couples in my news sample were positioned as discursive defenses against dominant ideologies of homosexuality as inherently inferior and deviant. Meanwhile, the "symbolic annihilation" of queer and unmarried gay identities continued (Gross, 2001), and challenges to heterosexism were scant (Barnhurst, 2003; Liebler et al., 2009). Gay marriage constructed as a suburban, middle- to upper-class, whites-only institution does little to interrupt heteronormative and classist definitions of "family values."

The "American game of assimilation," as Gross (2001) points out, can be a dangerous one, winnable only if marginalized groups play by the rules of dominant culture. Representations of gay marriages in the news—the couples, their talk of marriage, and their ceremonies—were constructed to appeal to a mainstream heteronormative audience. In doing so, news producers tapped into heterosexist ideologies by positioning these poster couples deserving of marriage vis-à-vis the wider community of unmarried gay, lesbian, bisexual, transgender, and queer individuals, who were implicitly cast as deviant, transgressive, and ultimately undeserving of full equality. As Walters (2001b) cautioned, public discourse surrounding the gay marriage debate "might grant visibility and acceptance to gay marrieds, but it will not necessarily challenge homophobia (or the nuclear family) itself; indeed, it might simply demonize nonmarried gays as the 'bad gays' (uncivilized, promiscuous, irresponsible) while it reluctantly embraces the 'good gays' who settle down and get married" (p. 349).

Indeed, these discourses surrounding identity politics and gay marriage specifically work to produce new forms of gay desire. As Walters (2001b) argues, one is not born with the innate yearning to partner in a state-sanctioned, monogamous, child-rearing relationship; these desires are part of a norm that multiple institutions of power construct and (re)produce. Enforcing this new *gay* desire to marry, *60 Minutes'* Bob Simon was seen in one segment running around the streets of the Castro, shoving a microphone in the faces of gay couples, asking about their intention to get married. Soliciting the opinions of one middle-age Caucasian male couple, Simon asks, "Are you guys going to get married?" Smiling, but clearly embarrassed and hesitant, one partner answered, "Hopefully he'll ask me sometime this year" (Hewitt, 2004, March 10). Ambivalence about marriage was transformed into the desire to marry. As one lesbian partner explained to the *New York Times,* economic pressures ultimately led her and her partner to marry. "The hard part is [that] the freedom to marry has become the pressure to marry has become the coercion to marry" (Belluck, 2004b, p. A19).

This coercion to marry is especially ironic and troubling considering how marriage is constructed as primarily a *female* desire. As the May 8, 2005, cover of the *New York Times* Sunday Styles section proclaims, "Even in gay circles, the woman wants the ring" (Bellafante, 2005). Of the first 5,400 couples wed in Massachusetts, the article reports, two-thirds have been lesbian couples. Why is the propulsion to wed largely a female desire? The article, citing sociologists and census statistics, argues that lesbian couples are more economically vulnerable, more likely to have children, and more likely to be susceptible to conformist cultural forces that promote marriage. As the pull quote on the inside page says, "Little girl dreams are the same, whether there's a man or a woman standing at the altar."

The fact that news discourses foreground lesbians as desiring of marriage, and that statistics bear out this pattern, ironically overlooks the problematic relationship between lesbianism and marriage's historic subordination of women—an institution "irrevocably mired in inequality and male dominance" (Walters, 2001b, p. 349). Interrupting the steady stream of hegemonic discourses, one article acknowledged the institution's problematic history. For one lesbian who was cited, deciding to marry was "a journey" to discover if she really wanted to be part of "an institution that comes out of a culture of ages-ago property exchange" (Belluck, 2004b, p. A19). Problematically, as chapter 4 details, these dominant media representations that promoted gay marriage as a female, suburban, and middle- to upper-class desire also largely excluded gays and lesbians of color, the poor, and the disenfranchised, those who would benefit the most from the institution's benefits and protections.

4. Gay Marriage Goes Prime-Time

Journalistic Norms Frame the Debate

> At the end of the day, I understand some of the pressure that is
> on the news media. "If it bleeds it leads." Sensationalism versus
> substance. They're worried about ratings. They're worried about
> market share. They're worried about their publisher being happy.
> And the gay rights issue is no different from any other issue that
> falls victim to that. If they can write it sensational, they will.
>
> —Cheryl, former president of the Human Rights Campaign

The July 13, 2003, edition of ABC's *Nightline* opened with what was considered a "shocking" image for prime-time news audiences at that time: a middle-age lesbian couple engaged in an open-mouth kiss during their wedding ceremony (Morris & Sloop, 2006; Sievers, 2004, July 13). The voice of one partner is dubbed over the video: "With this kiss, I thee wed." The image is immediately contrasted with a sound bite from a protester outside city hall shouting in anger, "What two men do when they get together, what two women do when they get together, is perverting the human body!" The next image is of a gay rights activist holding what appears to be an American flag, but rather than the traditional red and white stripes, this flag displays stripes of all colors of the rainbow. The activist is flanked on all sides by a half dozen police officers, thus signifying his threat to the social order and communicating the need for state authorities to preside over the gay nuptials taking place.

In the next shot another couple is shown, this time a middle-aged male couple at their wedding ceremony, reciting the traditional ceremonial language. This quiet, peaceful scene is followed by salacious images of protester aggression, filmed in the chaotic, eyewitness style of the television show *Cops*. The shaking camera and tense, close body posture of protesters gives the viewer the feeling that a physical fight is about to break out. As anti-gay protesters hold up homophobic signage, one gay activist shouts in anger, "You don't know about love!" These fast-paced images, which, all told, account for only the first 15 seconds of this *Nightline* episode, juxtapose celebratory shots of newly married lesbian and gay couples with angry and sometimes threatening demonstrations from conservative and religious protesters.

Despite attempts to "mainstream" gay marriage, as chapters 2 and 3 detail, activists in the marriage movement found themselves in many cases unable to disrupt what Edward Alwood (1996) refers to as the "long-standing anti-gay tone of the news media," or "straight news." Activists fell prey to the common pitfalls that have historically plagued reporting of social movements: coverage that radicalizes activist participants, oversimplifies and sensationalizes the cause, relies on imbalanced sourcing in an attempt to construct a balanced debate, and shortcuts the fullness of the community being covered.

In this chapter I examine journalistic storytelling techniques such as labeling, framing, sourcing, imagery, and graphics that were used to produce the gay marriage issue for mainstream news audiences in 2003–2004. What discursive strategies did mainstream news organizations employ to produce conflict in the news? How were labels and descriptive language used in news stories to validate historic homophobic discourses? How did privileging dominant political and religious sources work to dichotomize the debate and silence moderate perspectives? Finally, how did standard journalistic frames organize the marriage debate within "official" institutions of power?

This media analysis was informed by interviews with activists at the leading gay rights organizations whose job it was to shape coverage of gay and lesbian issues. This chapter not only reports on how the major national media organizations covered the gay marriage issue, but it also addresses how that coverage compared to the stated aims of activists on the front lines of the gay marriage debate. Embedded in their critique of press coverage are the challenges these social actors faced in trying to filter their messages and images through a commercial media industry. My interviewees discussed how journalistic definitions of authority, expertise, and "balance" created an uneven playing field, often pitting gay and lesbian spokespersons against unequal sources of influence from legal, medical, religious, and political authorities.

The Gay Marriage Battlefield: Producing Conflict in the News

Mass media scholars, sociologists, and political communication scholars alike have long shown how values of simplicity, conflict, drama, proximity, novelty, timeliness, and objectivity guide the journalistic production of issues and events. Those who study the production of news have not identified a conspiratorial, intentional bias on the part of reporters and editors. Rather, the demographic and ideological makeup of newsrooms and routine journalistic practices shape the content of news to privilege the powerful and maintain the status quo. As Todd Gitlin (1980) argues, "Simply doing their jobs, journalists tend to serve the political and economic elite definitions of reality" (p. 12).

There is nothing revelatory behind the notion that conflict drives news coverage. Professional norms, commercial imperatives, organizational deadline pressures, and the quest for audience attention in an increasingly fragmented media universe all drive reporters' "fatal attraction to the two-sided conflict" (Jamieson & Cappella, 2000, p. 329). The consequences, however, can be dire—for policy issues, political campaigns, and social movements alike. Framing complex issues as simple two-sided conflicts, and focusing on the strategies of the political and social players rather than on substantive issues, often obfuscates coverage of political campaigns, public policy issues, and controversial social issues. For example, journalistic values of simplicity, conflict, and scandal overshadowed the complexities of health-care policies in the early 1990s, ultimately leading to the failure of reform (Jamieson & Cappella, 2000.)

In the case of the same-sex-marriage issue, news coverage centered almost exclusively on the battle between two extreme conflicting sides—typically religious-conservative opponent groups contrasted with gay rights activists or couples desiring to marry—which led to problematic framing (e.g., "God vs. gays"). While the conflict frame provided a convenient and efficient narrative structure for journalists, it also cast participants into two fixed, opposing sides that silenced moderate perspectives. Furthermore, the disorder and chaos communicated through conflictual framing not only sensationalized the gay marriage issue but also worked to ascribe delinquency to gay marriage activists who posed a "threat" to the social order.

Both the qualitative textual analysis of media content and the quantitative content analysis of network television news stories confirmed that conflict was the go-to framing device during this time period, consistent across print and broadcast outlets, and present in nearly 80 percent of television news stories.[1] Specifically, three discursive strategies were central to the news production of conflict in same-sex-marriage stories: (1) reporters' use of sensationalistic language, often echoing conservative perspectives in their use of labels and language; (2) specific editing techniques that showed a clash of gay marriage proponents and protesters, juxtaposing conflicting images of gay and lesbian ceremonies with protesters picketing and praying; and (3) the selection and use of sources, those political, religious, legal, or activist figures positioned on opposing sides of the mediated debate.

Sensationalistic Labels and Language

In chapter 3 I highlighted how couples, families, and visual symbols were used to construct gay marriage as symbolically *similar to* heterosexual marriage. Paradoxically, the use of these visual symbols contradicted journalists' linguistic framing of gay marriage as radically *different from* traditional marriage. In terms of news coverage, the gay marriage issue was still in its relative infancy during this time period, seen through the lens of novelty, an abstraction. Perhaps not surprisingly, then, reporters' talk of gay marriage in the news often relied upon sensationalistic labels and language. In 68 percent of television news stories analyzed, reporters used language that played up conflict and dramatized the divisiveness of the issue. As one example, CBS reporter Jim Axelrod proclaimed on the July 13, 2004, broadcast of the *CBS Evening News,* "If you believe the polls, forget about abortion. Forget about gun control. The number one social issue this election year is gay marriage. And Americans are clear on it: against the idea of gay marriage 2 to 1" (Hewitt, 2004, July 13).

Oftentimes, journalists unwittingly echoed conservative perspectives when they talked about gay marriage as indicative of an overall modern social upheaval. For example, the introductory segment of the July 13, 2004, *Nightline* began with Ted Koppel solemnly telling his viewing audience, "Marriage in America is not just bouquets and champagne toasts anymore" (Sievers, 2004, July 13). In a similar vein, Barbara Walters's story of Rosie O'Donnell and Kelly Carpenter O'Donnell used video footage of their same-sex ceremony to contrast a traditional heterosexual ceremony, saying: "The bride didn't wear white. She didn't throw the bouquet. And the happy couple didn't fly off for a romantic honeymoon. But they did steal headlines across the country" (Sloan, 2005, April 8).

The March 10, 2004, edition of *60 Minutes* also defined gay marriage in terms of difference from the heterosexual institution when reporter Bob Simon described a scene outside the San Francisco city hall, proclaiming, "There are plenty of brides and plenty of grooms, but they don't marry each other!" (Hewitt, 2004, March 10). Later in the program Simon defined gay marriage as a "sudden and radical change to the culture." He also used linguistic markers to draw boundaries between those gays who want to marry and those who do not and, thus by inference, choose to live outside the norm of American society.

During in-depth interviews I conducted, several activist informants discussed how the simple and oftentimes subtle terminology that reporters used to cover LGBT people, and gay marriage specifically, worked to further radicalize and criminalize the activist community. Because news stories are derived from a heterosexist vantage point, the prejudicial language used to label gays and lesbians in the press is plentiful (Alwood, 1996). Several activists pointed out how even the predominant labels the news media used inaccurately framed gay marriage as a separate institution. One informant expressed the challenges of having to contend with the terminology that echoed throughout media and popular discourse: "'Gay marriage' sort of sets it apart and makes it sound like this is marriage that is different from the marriage that everyone else knows and understands. And that's in fact the antithesis of the point. The whole point is it's not different, it's not special, it's not a new institution. It's giving same-sex couples access to marriage" (Michael, Human Rights Campaign).

Activists sought to frame the issue using their preferred labels like "marriage equality," "equal marriage rights," or "marriage for same-sex couples" so that the public would understand that gay rights activists were not attempting to reinvent the institution, but simply working to expand existing marriage laws to include same-sex couples.

The propensity of sensationalizing language not only contributed to framing "gay marriage" as different from "real marriage," but from the perspective of my activist informants it also made it difficult to move beyond the "hype" and present the "deeper story" of gay and lesbian lives and families. Activist and former Massachusetts state senator Cheryl Jacques explained her struggle of being branded in the press as an openly gay politician, unable to escape the discursive labeling that Lisa Bennet (2000) writes has historically stigmatized gays and lesbians.

> I think some reporters are really in the dark ages. I remember when I was campaigning, and that's awhile ago, but it still happens: "Jaques, an avowed lesbian." "Jaques, an admitted lesbian." And I would call the reporter and say, "'An admitted lesbian'? Are you 'an admitted straight person'? Will you look at those words? It sounds like I'm an alcoholic or an admitted tax felon. Or 'an avowed lesbian.' Do you take a vow to be straight? . . . That makes me sound radical or militant. I'm just who I am, guys, and I'm just being truthful about it. I didn't take a vow!"

For many of my activist informants, the media frenzy that worked to sensationalize gay marriage as a hot-button issue that would sell more newspapers and drive ratings also took attention away from their work on other causes. As an out-lesbian political figure, Jacques faced difficulties in receiving press attention on any issue other than gay marriage. The conflict surrounding the subject became so pervasive that it constrained her ability to shift press attention to a host of other important issues she represented, reducing her work in the legislature and her entire campaign to a single cause. She complained of newspaper coverage the morning after a campaign debate: "I would see headlines: 'Jacques: Pro Gay Marriage.' And that was some sort of tiny little thing we had talked about in a whole discussion about economic policy and education policy and health care . . . And I'd think, here we go again. As if all I care about is gay marriage, when I spent two hours talking about everything else and one minute talking about gay rights. The editor knew that would make people read the article or would kind of jazz everybody up."

Frustrated by the sensational coverage, these informants who worked with the news media uniformly argued that their greatest hurdle was in packaging their story and their message in a condensed form that was fit for a highly competitive and commercialized media system. Referring to the waning attention span of American news audiences, one activist bemoaned, "We're a *USA Today* culture, not an NPR culture" (Chris, Log Cabin Republicans). Americans want their news packaged in fast, simple, consumable, bite-size portions, burdening social actors to tell their side of the story in the form of "a neat little sound bite." One activist explained the challenge of communicating a complex issue like gay marriage, in particular for condensed television news debates, in this way:

> It is really easy for our opponents to say, "We need to preserve traditional marriage. Marriage is good for our family. Every child should have a mother and a father." Even I hear that and I go, yeah, that's not a bad message. But we have to tell the deeper story. "Okay, not every child has a mother and a father . . . Not every father and mother are good parents. What kids really need is love and attention and nurture. And the ideal household is two loving, committed parents and the resources to raise that child." That's a hard message. It doesn't fit in a sound bite. (Cheryl, former president of the Human Rights Campaign)

Several other informants gave examples of the "deeper story" that they struggled to tell, one that the news media failed to cover. One activist referred to the coverage of the Federal Marriage Amendment (FMA) as "woefully insufficient," failing to report that under this new law, gays and lesbians would be excluded not only from marriage but from civil unions as well. He saw it as hypocritical that after calling for the passage of the amendment, President George W. Bush would go on morning talk shows and say he supported civil unions, touting his minimal tolerance for gay and lesbian relationships as his compromise position. Reporters failed to investigate the full reach of the FMA or to bring out the inconsistencies in the president's position.

Dueling Visuals Drive Conflict

Another way news organizations produced conflict was through the selection and juxtaposition of dueling images of activists, couples, and protesters. Oftentimes, images of "traditional" heterosexual wedding ceremonies were contrasted with same-sex couples' ceremonies to graphically communicate some sort of cultural shift brought about by gay marriage. For example, in the opening segment of the February 24, 2004, *Nightline* edition, viewers are presented with a black-and-white, cinematic-style image of a happy, young, heterosexual Caucasian couple kissing during what appears to be their marriage ceremony—she in a traditional lacy wedding gown, he in a black tuxedo (Sievers, 2004, February 24). The style of dress, hair, and filming has a 1950s look to it. As Ted Koppel narrates, "That was then, this is now," a barrage of images flashes across a split screen. Moving black-and-white images of heterosexual wedding ceremonies appear on the left side, juxtaposed with color video images of same-sex couples embracing and kissing during their apparent ceremonies on the right. In an energetic style of visual narration, each image appears for only a split second. Dueling sound bites are dubbed over this fast-paced "kiss-off" between straight couples and gay couples: a lesbian partner talking about what their marriage means to her, contrasted with President Bush and Senator Rick Santorum calling for a constitutional amendment to protect the institution. Through Koppel's narration, the use of fast-paced contrasting imagery, and the dubbed-in sound bites, the gay marriage issue is presented as dramatic, chaotic, and confusing, as if the terrain of marriage were undergoing seismic and violent shifts.

The fast-paced, same-sex-couple/angry-religious-protester dyad I described at the beginning of this chapter was a common way to represent the issue not only in television news but in print media as well. The inside spread of the *Newsweek* cover story that begs the question "Is gay marriage next?" features similar dueling images. The dominant image is of two women—one donning a traditional white wedding dress and veil, the other in a black tuxedo-like pantsuit—engaged in a passionate open-mouth kiss while onlooking supporters cheer and clap. The dueling image to the left is of an older white-haired man, holding a sign that reads, "Homosexuality, Hellfire, Sin," the words themselves graphically illustrated to appear as though they are on fire. In the foreground of the image, a blurred figure of a police officer once again subtly highlights the presence of state authority.

As a result, homophobic imagery and discriminatory language from conservative groups were given a stage, positioned as credible opposing viewpoints. Images of same-sex couples getting married were continuously

SAN FRANCISCO, CA: A member of the religious group Repent America demonstrates against same-sex marriages in front of a queue of gay and lesbian couples on their way to get married at San Francisco City Hall on February 20, 2004. (Photo by Hector Mata/AFP/Getty Images)

contrasted with opponents holding anti-gay signage that cited biblical verses and referenced religious imagery (also fueling the "God vs. gays" framing discussed later in this chapter and in chapter 5). The March 10, 2004, episode of *60 Minutes* featured protester signage that read, "Homosexuality is Sin," "Stop Destroying the Family," "This is Proof Homosexuals are Lawless," and "Adam & Eve not Adam & Steve" (Hewitt, 2004, March 10). Similarly, the July 13, 2004, *Nightline* featured signs proclaiming, "Homosexuals are possessed by demons," and showed footage of protesters wearing T-shirts with the word "homo" circled and crossed out with a bright red bar (Sievers, 2004, July 13).

In giving vitriolic rhetoric like this exposure on prime-time news programs, news producers publicize perspectives that criminalize and demonize homosexuality. As I argue in this next section, by selecting images and oppositional sources from religious conservatives on the far right, mainstream news organizations replayed historic homophobic stereotypes and provided a platform for extreme anti-gay discourses.

Balance and Objectivity: Sourcing the Debate

Who the news media select as sources and how their voices are presented has been the concern of a large body of scholarly research (see, for example,

Blumler & Gurevitch, 1995; Gans, 1979; Grabe & Zhou, 1999; Graber, 1997; Just, Crigler & Buhr, 1999; Sigal, 1973). Jay Blumler and Michael Gurevitch (1995) assert that when reporters cover issues, they tend to seek out field-defined official sources who can give them an authoritative perspective. The result is that "alternative definitions of social issues are then disadvantaged— either not represented at all, given short shrift, or labeled as 'interested' and 'biased'" (p. 30). It has been widely recognized that white, male, heterosexual, government-based "elite" or "official" sources dominate both television and print media, leaving little space for the voices of ordinary citizens (Graber, 1997). This research has shown that more than half, and often as high as three-quarters, of all news sources cited are local, state, national, and international government officials (Gans, 1979; Grabe & Zhou, 1999; Sigal, 1973). Journalists' heavy reliance on the narrowly defined "authoritative" viewpoint leaves little room for the voices of average citizens or social movement leaders attempting to challenge the political agenda of elites.

When it comes to coverage of gay issues, these routine journalistic standards often dictate that gay and lesbian people are pitted against opposing "official" sources from legal, medical, religious, and political authorities. Their lives are thus viewed through the lenses of psychiatrists, clergymen, and congressmen, but rarely from the perspective of their own community. This pattern emerged in the 1950s and '60s when gay people routinely appeared on panels with psychiatrists describing homosexuality as a mental illness, and it continued through the 1990s with military officials explaining the rationale behind the "Don't Ask, Don't Tell" policy. In short, in the news, gay people have historically "been the least important sources of information and opinion about their own lives" (Gross & Woods, 1999, p. 349).

In following standards of journalistic neutrality, reporters tend to seek out and give voice to the most dichotomous viewpoints on either side of an issue. Scholars who study social and political movements have shown how journalistic notions of objectivity, or presenting "both sides" of an issue as if there were only two viable alternatives to "choose" from, works to disadvantage social movement activists. By relying on sources from very different hierarchical power structures and pitting them against one another, journalists and editors produce binary divides that unwittingly marginalize activists seeking social reforms. In his canonical work on the antiwar movement in the 1960s, sociologist Todd Gitlin (1980) demonstrated how notions of journalistic "objectivity" often resulted in imbalanced sound bites—one from a rational-sounding, clean-cut authority figure and one from a disheveled, crazed-looking student "radical." In this way the news media recognize the alternative viewpoints of social movement actors but at the same time further marginalize and ridicule them.

Likewise, Alwood (1996) shows that the journalistic practice of objective reporting demands that reporters seek information from "verifiable" sources— "information from politicians, police, clergy, psychiatrists—historically society's most forceful antigay detractors" (p. 10). Lisa Bennet (2000) argues that coverage of gay and lesbian issues in the news media has been plagued by a "profound imbalance in the power and prestige of sources quoted" (p. 35). Her analysis of *Time* and *Newsweek*, spanning over 50 years of coverage of gay issues, found that reporters tended to accept at face value the opinions of traditional sources of power, including religious leaders, government officials, politicians, and celebrities. Reporters have historically been reluctant to question authoritative sources, ask for supporting evidence, or offer competing viewpoints. As Alwood (1996) writes, the journalistic strive for "balance" on controversial gay rights issues has only given "anti-gay fanatics a platform from which to profound their bigotry under the guise of providing 'the other side' . . . Although it would be unthinkable for journalists to interview a Ku Klux Klan member or a neo-Nazi for stories about African Americans or Jews—or to interview a misogynist for a story on women's rights—the media think nothing of routinely including demeaning and hateful remarks from bigots and antigay zealots in stories about gay rights" (p. 323).

In gay marriage stories, these same sourcing patterns persist, generally pitting anonymous same-sex couples and gay rights activists against collared religious figures and powerful political figures. Quantitative analysis of the sources cited in television news reports during this time frame found that while gay and lesbian couples and gay rights activists made up 16.8 percent and 8.2 percent, respectively, of the sources cited, political figures (27.4 percent), conservative activists (13.4 percent), religious and legal figures (8.3 percent), and the president and his spokespersons (10.6 percent) overshadowed gay perspectives (see table).

In positioning gay and lesbian couples against traditional sources of power and authority such as the president, congressmen, and respected religious leaders, the news media unwittingly created an uneven playing field in which gay perspectives were unable to compete in public discourse. As one example, the introductory segment of the July 13, 2004, episode of *Nightline* represented two conflicting sides of the debate in a way that was emblematic of overall coverage. The segment featured unidentified gay couples speaking about how much marriage means to them in contrast with state authorities like Senator Rick Santorum, who addressed Congress in a suit and tie, and argued passionately, "If you really care about preserving one man, one woman in a union called marriage, there is one sure-fire certain way to do it, and that is to vote for a constitutional amendment that does it" (Sievers, 2004, July 13).

Sources cited in television news stories about gay marriage, 2003–2004, with mean length of sound bite, in seconds.

Source Identity	%	N	Mean	SD
Political figure	27.4	90	7.98	4.66
Gay/lesbian couple	16.8	55	8.75	7.26
Conservative activist	13.4	44	10.14	7.61
President George W. Bush	8.5	28	9.07	6.48
Gay rights activist	8.2	27	9.44	5.03
Academic/legal/political analyst	7.6	25	10.84	3.58
Legal figure	4.3	14	8.93	5.92
Religious figure	4.0	13	9.54	5.09
Vox pop	3.0	10	4.60	1.96
White House representative	2.1	7	7.29	1.98
Other/undetermined	1.8	6	7.00	2.45
Gay ally	1.5	5	34.50	36.57
Uncoupled gay or lesbian citizen	0.6	2	6.00	.00
Journalist/reporter	0.6	2	7.00	2.83
Total	100	328	9.16	7.68

Note: "*N*" stands for the raw number of sources, "*Mean*" represents the average length of sound bite, in seconds, and "*SD*" represents the standard deviation, or how much variation existed from the mean value. The "gay ally" mean value of 34.50 seconds was largely skewed by one particular news story in which the grown 20-something daughter of a gay couple was granted over a minute and a half of speaking time (hence the high standard deviation as well). This source had just written a book about her experience growing up in a household with two (gay) fathers.

Reflecting this imbalance of power, *Nightline* continued by identifying the leader of the national movement against same-sex marriage, the key opponent of gay couples seeking marriage rights, as the president of the United States. Sound bites from the president solemnly addressing Congress or the American public were juxtaposed with celebratory images of couples' ceremonies. In 2004 and 2005 political and legal figures were rarely shown in support of equal marriage rights for gay couples, with the exception of openly gay Massachusetts congressman Barney Frank and San Francisco mayor Gavin Newsom. As chapter 5 highlights, coverage evolved in 2008–2010 as the proportion of politicians speaking on behalf of same-sex-marriage rights grew substantially, representing a maturation of the issue in political discourse.

Gay marriage opponents who were selected by reporters and editors to voice their opinions in the news—including religious leaders, conservative activists, and politicians—equated gay marriage with social disorder, pedophilia, and polygamy, painting an apocalyptic picture of a modern-day Sodom and Gomorrah. President George W. Bush, the most cited same-sex-marriage opponent at the time, argued in a sound bite repeated across several news texts, "The union of a man and woman is the most enduring

human institution . . . honored and encouraged in all cultures and by every religious faith" (Sievers, 2003, July 2). Several opponents rooted in the
fundamentalist Christian faith, like Randy Thomasson of the Campaign for
California Families, invoked the rhetoric of a slippery slope, commonly used
by the conservative right, and argued that it would be dangerous to create a
society in which you could marry whomever you love. Thomasson painted
a fear-provoking picture of a future America in which "children could be
marrying older men, the number of partners could number three or four in
a marriage" (Sievers, 2004, July 13).

Citing scripture and drawing from biblical references was also a routine
strategy used by opponents to define gay marriage as incompatible with the
norms of traditional marriage. Rev. Eugene Rivers, in his *Nightline* appearance,
quoted the gospel, saying God intended man and woman to "cleave together" to
raise a family. Linking marriage to procreation, thus solidifying the relationship
between legal partnering and parenting, was a rhetorical device that religious
figures commonly employed to define the cultural meaning and purpose of
marriage. As Reverend Rivers argued, marriage is essential "for the proper
rearing of children," stating that to have anything less than two parents—a
mother and a father—is categorically unfair to kids (Sievers, 2004, July 13).
A common fear of social conservatives, and an argument often used in news
discourse, is that equal marriage will allow gay couples to claim adoption rights
as well as opportunities to produce their own children through reproductive
technologies. The presupposition that marriage will *lead* to parenting, of course,
denies the multiple and far more common ways families are structured in the
United States today, including heterosexual married couples who choose not
to have children, single parents raising children on their own, and of course
heterosexual and same-sex couples who choose to raise children without getting married, just to name a few.

This rhetorical strategy that anchors marriage to child-rearing (and vice
versa) also ignores the existence of the hundreds of thousands of children
already living in gay households, those children who are not afforded the
same financial protections as heterosexual married households. According
to the 2010 census, on average, one-quarter of same-sex households included
children under 18, totaling 115,000 out of the 594,000 same-sex-couple households who reported. Nearly half of U.S. adoption agencies report that they
have placed a child with a gay or lesbian couple (Coontz, 2005, p. 275). Koppel does not challenge Rev. Rivers on the issue of raising children, nor does
he refer to any of these statistics about the number of children who were
living in gay households at the time. His silence on the subject once again
fails to address one of the most significant issues left out of the debate: how

to ensure that children growing up in same-sex-partner households, unmarried households, and single-parent households receive financial protections and health care coverage that are equal to those of children growing up in mixed-sex-married households.

Marriage equality activists were acutely aware of the potential pitfalls of being selected as a source in a news story, especially in talk-show-style debates. In their critique of media coverage, several of my interviewees described falling prey to the "media fallacy" of journalistic objectivity. They discussed what they saw as a structural problem in the news when, in following the path of least resistance, journalists constructed a two-sided debate in which the "gay voice" was almost always on the losing side. The routine media practice of constructing an "objective" binary often resulted in staging a point-counterpoint debate between a gay rights spokesperson and a religious leader, granting equal time to both sides. Several informants had experienced firsthand being thrown into a ring where they were sure to be the loser. Cheryl, then president of the Human Rights Campaign, described this common scenario.

> CNN calls. The Reverend Jerry Falwell is coming on to talk about the fact that gay people are bad and God doesn't support them. Will you come answer it? Will you counter it, Cheryl, gay rights activist for the leading gay rights organization? And I'd go and we'd do it. Then I started saying, this isn't right. America is loading their dishwasher and they're watching a reverend, a theologian, a biblical person (he's not really) talk about God and the Bible, and the counter isn't, you know, Bishop Gene Robinson or Rabbi David Saperstein or Priest John Blow or Minister Kevin Jones. It's gay rights activist Cheryl Jacques? Like, hello! I'm losing that the moment I walk in the door.

Further tipping the debate, reporters also tended to accept those oppositional sources of power at face value, leaving their claims unquestioned. In one example, Cheryl described her frustration when journalists would allow opposing sources like religious figures to tell what were, in her view, unsupported "blatant lies" and not calling them on it. Religious spokespeople like Jerry Falwell and Tony Perkins would say on television that instead of fighting for marriage equality, gay couples should simply recreate the benefits and protections of marriage by hiring a good lawyer. However, not only is that kind of legal representation inaccessible to most couples, but as Cheryl said, there is no lawyer who has the power to rewrite federal tax policy and secure social security survivor benefits to an unwed partner. Claims like this often went undisputed by reporters, inaccurately portraying the push for marriage equality as unsubstantiated and unnecessary.

Religious figures were also common sources in news stories, always opposing gay rights and often questioning the very legitimacy of gay and lesbian
people. For example, in the previously cited July 13, 2004, *Nightline* episode,
Rev. Rivers of the Massachusetts Pentecostal Church used biblical and normative arguments to claim that redefining marriage for gay couples would
personally threaten his heterosexual marriage. He argued further that the
core feature of civilization is the joining together of a man and woman and
that allowing same-sex couples to form unions and have families is dangerous for society.

Constructing the debate in this way led to a deeply rooted pattern that
positioned gay and lesbian couples in direct opposition to religious values
and "morals," ultimately relying on a simplistic but inaccurate framing device,
"God vs. gays." Michael of the Human Rights Campaign referred to this as
an unfair co-opting of religious values by a small group of individuals who
claim a monopoly on morals. Marriage activists found themselves constantly
struggling to shift the conversation to one in which religious values were a
part of the gay voice, not set in opposition to it. They sought to create spaces
in the media debate for supportive religious leaders to speak out in favor of
same-sex marriage. As I discuss in chapter 5, this prevalent "God vs. gays"
framing in 2003–2004 set the tone for later coverage in 2008–2010, in part
pressuring gay rights organizations to hire new faith-based staff positions
and develop outreach efforts in religious communities.

This predominant framing by the media became especially problematic
when religious narratives conflated with racial representations, often featuring religious African American leaders in a debate against Caucasian
gay rights activists. Media personnel, accustomed to habit, constrained by
deadlines, and limited to a "stock" bank of sources, often fell back on this
common sourcing pattern. As one activist expressed it, in a reporter's mind,
"If I want an opposition viewpoint, oh, right, let me get a black minister" who
will "shout hellfire and brimstone." For example, Arlene of the Massachusetts
Gay and Lesbian Political Caucus told the story of when she was, in her view,
"set up" by a cable news show in the 1980s to debate an African American
minister in front of a mostly black middle-class conservative audience. It
hit her as she walked on stage that she was fighting a losing battle, a "black
handsome minister against this white Jewish lesbian."

The lack of black and religious spokespeople speaking on behalf of gay
rights, and often cast as opposed to gay rights, complicated gay organizations'
strategic attempts to frame gay marriage as a civil rights issue. As chapter 5
details, the "blacks vs. gays" frame became especially problematic in 2008
in the context of the election of Barack Obama and, at the same time, the

passing of Proposition 8 in California that banned gay marriages in the state. As Arlene explained it, when "you've got a bunch of white gay people saying it's a civil rights issue, it's meaningless and resented by the black community for understandable reasons."

One of the biggest challenges for gay marriage activists, then, became to create a more diverse bank of sources for media outlets, in particular supportive religious and civil rights leaders, who would speak in favor of marriage equality. Cognizant of the visual impact of religious symbols in this debate, Arlene, who was responsible for lining up media spokespeople, went as far as coaching supportive religious leaders to "dress the part." She insisted her religious spokespeople wear the visual adornments of the *kippah* (yarmulke) or the clerical collar. Frustrated by leaders who would make media appearances in casual dress, she would tell them, "'Come on, guys, you just diminish your value to us if you're not wearing—you've gotta wear that little clerical collar. That's the big sign.' In this debate, 20 years later, we needed as many collars coming out, saying the right thing, as that image buster: the revelatory notion that in fact religion did support us."

Further, recognizing the limits of her status as a "white Jewish lesbian" in this debate, Arlene feared that her very presence in the media contributed to the stereotype that all gay activists—and, for that matter, all gay people—were white and privileged. She therefore took a step back as the primary media spokesperson for her organization in order to highlight the voice, perspective, and image of her co-chair, Gary, an African American male. "So whenever the press would call, I'd say—if it was broadcast, if it was TV—'Talk to Gary.' And if it was print media, I'd still say, 'Talk to Gary.' But I'd say, 'Gary, be sure to tell them you're black.' Otherwise, gay activist, everyone pictures white."

So although gay and lesbian activists and couples were featured in prominent, mainstream news stories, their presence was mostly restricted to two-sided debates against conventionally "straight" voices and perspectives. Coverage of the marriage issue, in other words, was imbalanced, sustaining the long-standing pattern of inequality in the power, prestige, and prominence of the sources cited (Alwood, 1996; Bennet, 2000). Conservative activists, political and legal analysts, religious figures, legal sources, and even the president himself were allotted more time to speak in news reports than were gay and lesbian citizens. As the previous chapter reported, of the couples who visually appeared in television news stories, only 20 percent were given the opportunity to speak at all. Coverage of the gay marriage issue continued the well-documented pattern of granting often-heterosexist opposing sources from legal, medical, religious, and political institutions the opportunity to "talk about gay people, rather than allowing them to speak for themselves" (Gross & Woods, 1999, p. 349). As chapter 5 details, as the issue matured, the activist community continued to struggle over how best to represent pro-gay perspectives in mediated discourses and gain support from the "moveable middle."

Framing the Story: Journalistic Frames and Activist-Preferred Frames

From underreporting the numbers at gay rights marches and events (by relying on "official" police estimates rather than those of organizers) to downplaying and trivializing the 1969 Stonewall riots credited with sparking the gay liberation movement, scholars have argued that the mainstream media has participated in disparaging and marginalizing the efforts of gay activists (Alwood, 1996; Gross & Woods, 1999).

As a long line of mass communications scholarship has shown (see chapter 1), the ways in which news personnel frame issues, events, and communities shapes how news audiences come to interpret those issues and communities. To make sense of extraordinary events, and to be able to do their jobs efficiently, journalists organize events around major societal themes, frames, or conflicts that offer "definitions of social reality" (Tuchman, 1976, p. 94). Frames operate as "organizing principles that are socially shared and persistent over time, that work symbolically to meaningfully structure the social world" (Reese, 2001, p. 11). Mainstream news media become an important site of struggle over framing, as groups in power and those attempting to have a voice in the debate compete to have their perspectives and definitions dominate.

Gay rights activists interviewed for this study discussed the challenges they faced when attempting to frame issues in the press, often having to compete with oppositional frames like "God vs. gays" as well as standard journalistic frames like novelty and conflict. The increased press attention on gay and lesbian issues in the past decade meant that leaders of the gay rights movement had to be concerned with framing the message. My analysis here is thus driven by concerns on the part of both activists and scholars over the dominant framing of gay activism and gay issues, which has historically derived from a "straight" heterosexist vantage point.

Reporters have the ability to create and access a number of effective framing devices when covering an issue like same-sex-marriage rights, the most common ones being: (1) legalistic/legislative, analyzing the impact of the various court cases surrounding the issue, and how particular judges may vote; (2) political, or "horse-race-style" coverage of public opinion polls on the issue and how gay marriage may impact the various senatorial campaigns and the presidential election; (3) as a civil rights issue, articulating with language and images of former civil rights movements; or (4) as a love story, a human-interest, couple-centered frame that reports on a same-sex couple's journey of meeting, falling in love, and ultimately attempting to marry. These framing devices, as previously indicated, do not "emerge" organically, but are established by professional journalistic norms. These frames are not exhaustive nor are they mutually exclusive; more often than not, several frames were used to structure a single news story.

For example, often in conjunction with the dominant conflict framing, a majority of news stories framed gay marriage as a *political* issue (67.7 percent) and as a *legal* issue (60.2 percent). Since the same-sex-marriage debate often shared the same news cycle with electoral campaigns (e.g., the 2004 presidential campaign), the dominance of political framing was not surprising. This framing device typically reported on how the issue was likely to affect upcoming races for Congress or the presidency. The political frame was also used to report on how voters were likely to decide on a variety of future referendums or ballot initiatives on same-sex-marriage rights, considering the issue was on the ballot in 11 states during the 2004 election, three states during the 2008 election, and four states during the 2012 election. Political figures were prominent players in this story framing—figures like President George W. Bush, Senator John Kerry, Senator Bill Frist, and former Democratic governor and 2004 presidential candidate Howard Dean. Visuals featured images of the candidates, as well as b-roll of the House or Senate floor, where congressional leaders were debating the Federal Marriage Amendment.

Legal framing reported on the issue in the legislative realm, often interpreting the legal impact or meaning of particular court cases—for example, the *Lawrence* case, which repealed anti-sodomy laws, or the historic *Goodridge* case, which legalized gay marriages in Massachusetts. These stories often cited legal scholars and constitutional law experts to report on "what the court said" or "how the court decided." Legal stories might also report on how a court is likely to vote and the legislative maneuvering on the part of activists (both gay rights and conservative) to bring a case forward.

While less common than standard journalistic conflictual, political, and legal framing, many stories also contained the activist-preferred frames of same-sex marriage as a civil rights issue, or as simply a love story. As chapter 2 discusses, these frames came to represent a fundamental divide among those in the marriage equality movement about how best to represent their cause. The majority of activists in the gay community during this time frame saw marriage as an issue of equal rights, similar to nondiscrimination in the workplace, equal access to health care and education, and so forth. But other activists were concerned that "rights" language would turn off news audiences, insisting that marriage was not a set of "unemotional" rights, obligations, and responsibilities, but the ultimate expression of universal "romantic love."

Stories that framed the issue along the lines of *romantic love* (present in 25.8 percent of stories) typically focused on the story of a couple and recounted their journey of meeting, falling in love, and eventually seeking marriage rights. Their love story was presented similarly to how a heterosexual love story would be told, often including still photos of the couple from a time when they met and interviewing the couple about what brought them together. Discourses of homosexual romantic love, popularized in films like *Brokeback Mountain* (2006), asks perceived "straight" audiences to empathize with the couple and see their love and their relationship as no different from their own.

Employed twice as often as romantic love framing, *civil rights* framing (present in 53.5 percent of stories) appeared to be more resonant to journalists, who structured stories within dominant paradigms of inequality and discrimination.

BOSTON, MA: Two women protest in favor of same-sex-marriage rights outside the Massachusetts State House on March 29, 2004, in Boston. Inside, the state legislature was entering the third round of debates over a possible constitutional amendment banning same-sex marriage but allowing civil unions. News coverage of the gay marriage issue often evoked civil rights discourses. (Photo by Michael Springer/Getty Images)

In fact, activists who promoted civil rights framing over love insisted that mainstream media outlets and news audiences were not ready to embrace stories of homosexual romance on the same level as "straight love." In fact, in the words of one activist, romantic framing would only contribute to the "ick factor." As she put it, promoting gay marriage as an extension of love would never "sell" to straight audiences (Arlene, Massachusetts Gay and Lesbian Caucus).

News personnel relied on civil rights framing to focus on issues of discrimination, fair and equal treatment of all citizens, and the rights and protections that marriage equality affords gay and lesbian couples. News organizations made deliberate attempts—through the language reporters used, the social actors they cited, and the imagery they created and selected—to link gay marriage with the civil rights movement of African Americans, specifically to articulate with the battle to legalize interracial marriage in the 1960s. Some stories compared the court decisions that legalized gay marriage with other "milestone" cases like *Brown v. Board of Education,* which ended racial segregation in public schools. The May 18, 2004, edition of the *New York Times* ran a front-page story the day after Massachusetts became the first state to allow same-sex marriage, writing, "Gay rights activists hailed this day, which fell on the 50th anniversary of the Supreme Court decision *Brown v. Board of Education,* as an occasion that evoked the triumphs—and the social vindication—of the civil rights era" (Belluck, 2004a, p. A1). Stories employing the civil rights frame equated discrimination against gays and lesbians with discrimination against racial and ethnic minorities. In a rare instance of citing a person of color speaking on behalf of gay rights, one television news story included a sound bite from an African American congresswoman saying she knew the pain of discrimination and therefore could not vote to ban same-sex marriages.

Social and political supporters of same-sex marriage cited in the media drew connections between the fight for marriage equality and previous civil rights struggles, such as women's suffrage and interracial marriage. One recently married lesbian interviewed on *60 Minutes* said, "For me it feels like the option to get on the front of the bus as a lesbian . . . as opposed to the back of the bus" (Hewitt, 2004, March 10). Equal rights framing was a predominant strategy used by marriage proponents, especially by straight allies. Consider what San Francisco mayor Gavin Newsom told *Nightline*'s Ted Koppel to explain why he defied California law to issue same-sex marriage licenses: "In 1958, there was polls showing as high as 96 percent of whites in this country were opposed to interracial marriages. It took 'til 1967, in *Louving v. Virginia,* to end that practice in 16 states, to allow blacks to marry whites, whites to marry Asians and the like. If we wait for the right time, we'll never advance the cause for any discrimination in this country" (Sievers, 2004, July 13).

These civil rights discourses referred to gays and lesbians as minorities without equal rights. For example, one article from *USA Today* reported how the same-sex-marriage debate was moving into the workplace as gay couples demanded the same health insurance and other benefits that were offered to married couples. As one recently married lesbian told *USA Today,* "I'm going to continue to speak with them [my employers] about why they don't offer us the same rights. Now that I'm married, I'm more aware of all the rights we've been missing out on" (Armour, 2004).

Beyond the use of language and sourcing, news producers selected specific imagery to associate marriage equality for gay and lesbian couples with the struggle to legalize interracial marriages. The very presence of mixed-race couples used in photographs and television news stories alluded to the similarity between the movements. Indeed, it is telling that the only time we saw gay and lesbian people of color represented on the marriage issue was as part of a mixed-race couple. Often their statements and story framing made no linguistic references to interracial marriage, but the very use of their images served as visual reminders of the historic (and, for some, present-day) social taboos surrounding interracial marriage.

As I argued earlier in this chapter, the issue of same-sex marriage was largely framed within the standard journalistic frame of "conflict." Other framing devices used to tell the story confined the issue within "official" institutions of power that have historically criminalized and marginalized the gay community—politics (political), the courts and the police (legal), and the church (religious). Still, gay rights activists appeared to have met their stated objectives in promoting the issue as a civil rights issue or, alternately, as a love story. While the activist-preferred frames of civil rights and romantic love did not dominate in news stories about gay marriage, they were employed in more than half and more than a quarter of news stories, respectively. Again, the presence of these frames does not indicate that they were dominant, but almost always used in conjunction with several other frames. Nevertheless, the prevalence of both civil rights and romantic love framing indicates at the very least that activists were able to influence the story structures and encoded meanings of news narratives.

Conclusion: Gay Marriage Packaged for Prime-Time Audiences

By drawing our attention to the routine practices journalists used to produce the issue of same-sex marriage, this chapter revealed how media attention condensed the debate to a two-sided conflict that silenced moderate and secular perspectives. Media coverage also reduced the broader gay rights agenda to a single-issue movement. This media analysis indicates that while gays and lesbians—almost always shown as couples—were visually resonant in news stories, they were rarely given the opportunity to offer their own perspectives on this critical community issue.

In reporting on the gay marriage debate, the news media sustained the long-standing pattern of imbalance in the power, prestige, and prominence of the sources they cited (Alwood, 1996; Bennet, 2000). Reporters' reliance on unbalanced sourcing not only privileged but also rendered credible and innocuous insidious anti-gay imagery and historic homophobic discourses.

Analysis of the sources cited indicated how the debate was restricted to conventionally "straight" perspectives, continuing to grant power and prominence to authoritative (and often oppositional) sources from legal, religious, and political communities. While gay and lesbian couples and gay rights activists were consistently cited in news reports, political figures, conservative activists, religious figures, and the president himself dominated the debate and were allowed more time to speak than were gay and lesbian citizens. Those couples, the ones who had the most at stake, were given the least amount of time to tell their story. Gay and lesbian citizens were given a shorter sound bite, speaking less often and granted less time, than other sources speaking on their behalf, such as straight allies and gay rights activists.

As these findings reveal, gay and lesbian people in the news continued to appear more as "image bite" than "sound bite" (Bucy & Grabe, 2007; Grabe & Bucy, 2009). For the most part, the couples who served as the dominant visual focus of news stories contributed little to the linguistic content of the stories. In these television narratives, gay and lesbian couples seem to be granted the status of visual ornamentation. They are largely seen and not heard, and audiences are told very little about them. In the vast majority of these news reports, 82 percent of the time, the couples remained unidentified.

Considering the power of these visual narratives, this analysis was intensely concerned with who was represented, how they appeared, and what they were shown doing. On this issue the community was no longer "othered" or "exoticized" in stereotypical ways (such as gay bar life or pride parades), but instead was shown visually conforming to dominant, normative definitions of marriage and family. This suggests that in the battle over images, gay rights activists seemed to have met their stated goals of presenting the new face of gay and lesbian people in America: couples getting married, raising their children, or simply walking their dogs in what appeared to be a quiet, middle-class suburban neighborhood. Gay and lesbian people in the news almost exclusively appeared as couples. Their visual representations, once centered on urban street life; dark, seedy bars; and leather festivals, were arguably transformed in news stories about marriage, and gay and lesbian life became domesticated in typically heteronormative ways.

Therefore, the strategic communications and public relations arm of the gay rights movement, still in its relative infancy, appeared to have met its stated objectives in at least two ways. First, although proving a causal relationship is beyond the scope of this work, activists seemed to be successful in framing the debate principally as a civil rights issue and secondarily as a story of love. These findings suggest that activists who sought to control how the gay marriage issue was defined in the news media were able to assert their preferred framing devices.

Second, by promoting certain visuals over others, and producing their own imagery to accompany news stories, activists were able to provide new, "reformed" representations of gay and lesbian life. But activists also spoke of the continued struggle to visually represent the diversity of their community in news reports. According to some, it was difficult to line up racially diverse voices in the gay marriage conversation, as many people of color in their community remained closeted. Interestingly, media analysis indicated that while couples of color (where both partners were from a racial minority group) did not speak at all in television news reports, interracial couples spoke nearly twice as long in sound bites as did their Caucasian counterparts. This finding suggests that news producers privileged the perspectives of biracial couples, potentially alluding to previous civil rights struggles for interracial marriage.

As activists recognized, doing battle over marriage in the mainstream media meant conforming to the rules of news making. Conflict-driven, sensationalistic coverage forced activists to package their message into condensed sound bites for increasingly fractured news audiences. As chapter 5 details, these framing strategies and sourcing patterns from 2003 to 2004 set the stage for future reporting in 2008–2010, ultimately leading to internal debates and external conflicts in the wake of losing Proposition 8.

5. Speaking Out

Representing Gay Perspectives in News Discourse

On November 6, 2008, as CNN's Anderson Cooper described, "anger spilled into the streets" as demonstrators protested the passage of California's Proposition 8 (Doss, 2008, November 6). By a slim margin, 52 percent of the state's voters approved the controversial ballot measure that reversed the earlier state supreme court decision, once again making same-sex marriages in California illegal. The Prop 8 measure represented the most expensive campaign outside of the presidential contest and set a new record for spending on a social policy initiative. The "Yes on 8" campaign, seeking to ban gay marriages in the state, raised $39.9 million; Prop 8 opponent groups (the "No on 8" campaign) raised $43.3 million.

Alongside the victory of former Illinois state senator Barack Obama, U.S. news media fixed their attention on the passage of Proposition 8, what my activist informants described as a monumental loss for the gay rights movement. Mainstream news outlets led the evening broadcasts with protester footage of angry crowds shouting in unison, "Equal Rights," "No more H8!" and "Don't ask for equality. Demand it." That evening, CNN opened its newscast with an amateur video of police officers dragging a protester across a concrete sidewalk and pummeling the activist with sticks in the middle of the street. CNN's Cooper solemnly described the scene: "People are taking to the streets angry tonight over having their chance to marry be taken away."

With reportedly half of the "Yes on 8" funds raised by a campaign organized by the Mormon Church, many protests targeted the Church of Jesus Christ of Latter-Day Saints. In Los Angeles activists blocked off part of Santa Monica Boulevard, chanting, "Shame on you! Shame on you!" outside the Mormon headquarters there. Video and still photographs featured protester signage such as "Mormon Hate Leave Our State," "Church of Latter Day Hate," and "Take your magic undies off my civil rights."

The Prop 8 passage, of course, coincided with the victory of the country's first African American presidential candidate, and pundits and journalists alike immediately began to make connections between the two events, bandying about the "70 percent" statistic. With a high percentage of African American voters turning out to support Obama, and a reported 70 percent of them voting for the ban on same-sex marriage rights, reporters as well as political analysts were quick to attribute the gay movement's loss to the Obama victory.

For those activists working inside the movement, losing the California ballot initiative was not only "shocking" but also, as my informant Patrick put it, "a lost opportunity of historical proportions, and it'll be a lot harder to win again in the future." For some, the defeat was a wake-up call for the movement, as "a lot of gay people repented of their complacency and their failure to get engaged [in the movement]." As Evan explained it, "There are many people, particularly young people—gay as well as non-gay—who had grown up in an era of, 'We're winning.' And, oh, my God, we didn't win. And in California."

The Prop 8 vote—and the myriad legislative twists and turns that followed—served as a catalyst that propelled the same-sex-marriage controversy into the media spotlight once again, this time within fluctuating political contexts and shifting public understandings of the issue. Moreover, these battles waged over Proposition 8 in California and Question 1 in Maine the following year ultimately led to tensions over media representations and campaign strategies. In the view of several of my informants, movement leaders had shot themselves in the foot. Gay rights activists faced internal conflicts over the role of gay couples in news stories, the reliance on "straight allies" as spokespersons, and the use of images in campaign materials and media narratives.

In this chapter I report on the findings from activist interviews I conducted in 2010 and 2011, which included a return to many of the informants I spoke with in 2005. I interviewed a total of 20 individuals during this time period, including representatives from nine additional organizations that had become prominent voices in national news coverage since 2005: Lambda Legal; the Gay and Lesbian Alliance Against Defamation; Marriage Equality New York; the Victory Fund; Gay and Lesbian Activists Alliance; Parents, Families, and Friends of Lesbians and Gays; Equality California; National Center for Lesbian Rights; and the Family Equality Council. I conducted and analyzed these interviews, pairing them with news coverage of these events beginning in 2008, in order to reveal how media narratives, movement strategies, and activist perspectives evolved over time.

For comparative purposes, I selected a similar sample of news stories for this time period, from 2008 through 2010, with an emphasis on prominent, large-circulation news magazines, television news transcripts, and leading television evening news programs. In total this analysis included 43 articles from the print edition of national news magazines *Time, Newsweek,* and *U.S. News & World Report* (before it ceased its print edition); 20 television transcripts from the evening news broadcasts of NBC, CBS, ABC, and CNN; and an additional 28 video telecasts of network evening news programs from the Vanderbilt Television News Archive (for a total of 108 minutes of television news coverage). I employed textual analysis to examine the journalistic devices that produced dominant meanings of the controversial issue, including the prevalent frames, sourcing patterns, photographic and graphic images, moving images, voice-over narration, and visual representations of married couples and the LGBT community more broadly.

Since gay marriage had first captured the public imagination in 2003 and 2004, coverage of the issue had evolved considerably: gay marriage was no longer particularly novel, and it was no longer an abstraction. As chapter 1 recounts, this time period underwent a tremendous amount of political and legislative transformations. At the start of this project in 2003, only one state—Massachusetts—had legalized gay marriages. By 2011 five additional states—Iowa, New Hampshire, Connecticut, Vermont, and New York, as well as the nation's capital, had legalized marriage for same-sex couples. National public opinion polls continued to show growing support for gay marriage. Most informants in 2010 discussed the maturation of the issue in the press as a "tremendous amount of progress" in a relatively short period of time. Moreover, these continuing battles, whether won or lost, had, as Evan put it, fueled the movement for marriage equality by pushing "the conversation and the understanding and the center of gravity politically forward." Citing the "numbers of non-gay people who have taken this on as their cause," Evan and several other activists indicated that they were energized by the momentum.

Nevertheless, the evolving journalistic lenses for communicating the story also presented new challenges for the movement. As this chapter highlights, despite an overall more favorable tone and nuanced coverage of the issue, activists faced problematic framing devices that unfairly pitted communities of color against the LGBT community. Media outlets continued to look to religious leaders as "obvious" oppositional sources on gay rights. Furthermore, as interviews with movement leaders indicated, internal disagreements over how best to represent pro-gay perspectives in the media and gain support from the "moveable middle" divided the movement.

A Shift in Attitude: A More "Favorable," "Pro-Gay" Tone

From an activist perspective, journalistic attitudes shifted as the issue matured in public discourse. In the mid-1990s and into the early 2000s, coverage of the issue was seductively novel, and as chapter 4 argues, sensationalistic, following what Kate referred to as a "freak show mentality." Gay marriage "seemed like an anathema to many of the reporters covering it." Gay marriage wasn't just an abstraction; it was absurd. As Kate explained, "These weren't seen as real relationships or enduring families. There wasn't any sense that the reporter covering the stories saw themselves reflected in what they were covering. There was this sort of alien feature to it."

As the issue evolved in news discourses and in the larger public sphere, however, these standard journalistic lenses of novelty and deviance were less applicable in coverage of the gay marriage issue than they had been five or ten years earlier. The movement's project to mainstream and normalize marriage equality worked to some extent because those images and narratives of same-sex nuptials had become so ubiquitous. Evan explained it this way: "Five states have marriage. They haven't been washed away. There have been no locusts. Their divorce rates are the lowest in the country. Families are thriving. Gays didn't use up the marriage licenses. So people can now see with their own eyes that the scare tactics and the claims are just not true."

In 2010 and 2011, my activist informants argued that the changes in the tone of the coverage came from issue maturation; the American public had had time to "get used" to the idea, eliminating the relative "absurdity" and "default opposition" in many people's minds. By 2010 gay marriage was no longer a foreign construct. Michael explained, "There are a couple of things striking about it from a coverage perspective [in 2010]. One is it looked so normal. There were two people standing up in front of a crowd. There's a minister. There's some flowers. And, frankly, it's something we've worked really hard to achieve."

One of the most significant shifts in coverage was in the declining role of oppositional sources. In much of the early coverage surrounding the passage of Proposition 8 in California, for example, it was gay marriage opponent groups who were marginalized. Commonly, spokespersons for conservative groups were given short shrift: a four- to five-second sound bite in a two-minute-long story. In this time period, as opposed to previous coverage in 2003–2004, reports nearly exclusively *began* with the "gay voice," foregrounding gay and lesbian couples, gay rights activists, allies, and even supportive politicians (who were largely absent from the debate in 2004). Gay marriage opponent groups still maintained a presence in news stories, but their perspectives were often positioned at the end of the story, sometimes given the last word but often sidelined.

As one example, the May 15, 2008, *CBS Evening News* coverage highlights an overall celebratory tone in reporting on the California Supreme Court's decision that, at least temporarily, reinstated legal marriage for same-sex couples (Kaplan, 2008, May 15). The story opened on a large crowd of gay and lesbian partners, including several plaintiff couples, cheering and happily proclaiming before news crews, "Now I can finally marry my partner of 15 years!" and "We can't wait to get married." The story focused empathetically on the plight of gay and lesbian couples who have been navigating the legal twists and turns of marriage over the past several years. Producers cut to a shot from 2004 of one hopeful couple standing in line when the county clerk's office was ordered to stop issuing marriage licenses. The lesbian couple's disappointment was palpable; they cried out. At the end of the story, a leader from the oppositional Protect Marriage organization was asked by the reporter, "What's wrong with legalizing gay marriages in California?" In a three-second sound bite, the leader responded by simply saying, "The court has overstepped its bounds."

Most stories repeated this pattern, beginning with couples celebrating outside the courthouse en masse when the decision was announced, screaming, shouting, and jumping up and down amid a sea of supporters and television news cameras. Oppositional perspectives are acknowledged but appear more as journalistically obligated afterthoughts tacked on to the end of the story.

Similarly, in the round of coverage surrounding the passage of Prop 8 six months later, opponent groups were ostensibly overshadowed by pro-gay perspectives such as disappointed couples, shocked but determined LGBT activists, and even supportive politicians and legislators. This is not to imply that gay marriage opponent groups were silenced. On the contrary, as the next section highlights, oppositional rhetoric became increasingly heated as the news cycle continued. But in this round of coverage, these groups were granted less time to offer their opinions, and their perspectives were typically placed deeper into the story, more in a defensive posture rather than an offensive one.

This shift in tone represents a potential reversal in sourcing patterns. As chapter 4 highlighted, in 2004 the debate was dominated by conventionally "straight," often anti-gay, perspectives such as conservative groups and opposing political leaders. By 2010 the movement leaders and spokespersons I interviewed, many of whom had been working on this issue for decades in

WEST HOLLYWOOD, CA: Same-sex-marriage supporters listen to speeches during a rally to celebrate the ruling to overturn Proposition 8 on August 4, 2010. A federal judge overturned California's controversial Proposition 8, a same-sex-marriage ban, finding it unconstitutional. (Photo by Kevork Djansezian/Getty Images)

the press, referred to this overall "pro-gay" tone in coverage as a "sea change." Gay rights activists and media relations experts argued that over time their work to humanize the issue, employing the largely assimilatory strategies discussed in chapter 3, influenced journalistic attitudes and narratives. As Kate explained, "[Eventually] the reporters covering the story are like, 'Okay, remove the sexual orientation element and this is my next-door neighbor. These are my cousins. This is my daughter and her husband.' If you can get the media starting to identify, then they tell the story in a way that all of a sudden makes it not seem like a freak show but makes it seem like . . . 'This family is like other families.'"

Additionally, professional gay rights organizations themselves took more of a backseat in news coverage. Their relative absence as sources reflects a shift in media coverage and movement strategy (Barnhurst, 2003). Overall my activist informants received fewer media requests to do talk-show-style debates, the kind of interviews that prevailed in the earlier round of coverage, and were less inclined to grant those requests. Several activists like Kate and Cheryl told me they now avoid doing debate-style interviews, especially on "conservative media" broadcasts like the Christian radio program *Focus on the Family*, refusing to engage in disputes over whether gay people are "sinners." Activists strategically focused less on "talking heads" and more on the people directly affected by marriage laws, sending reporters to couples and families when media requests were received. As Marissa, a gay rights attorney, said, "If our [litigation] clients are quoted, it is a successful story."

Despite an increasingly favorable tone, many informants pointed out how mainstream news coverage still often adopted the language of the far right and failed to investigate what they referred to as "bogus claims" from the other side. As I explain in this next section, while opponent groups were getting less time and space in the news, their claims and rhetoric were more heated, controversial, and vitriolic. As Evan explained, "The anti-gay forces, realizing they're losing, have, in their—one hopes—last throes, really ratcheted up their game," building a vast infrastructure to channel money into anti-gay causes and raising tens of millions of dollars in California and Maine to pass restrictive gay marriage measures. This strategy of targeting and circulating messages to narrower but more attuned viewers was made ever more possible by the increasing polarization of news audiences.

Anti-Gay Sources in a Fractured Media World

In this round of coverage, activists faced an increasingly ideologically fragmented media universe. With fewer shared central media outlets that operate as the "defined public space" for audiences, activist informants said it was harder to conclusively win an argument. Because there is no centralized arena, with every story and in every media interview, "you're always talking to somebody else." Evan, as well as several other activists, discussed how the changing media universe made it more difficult to control the message. "The way in which the media world has evolved, it's much easier for people to channel their own message stream to their own people, and there's less serious robust journalism that will really challenge garbage. It all gets put forward and it all finds an audience."

In echoing the perspectives of the far right, many media reports ended up leaving egregious claims unquestioned, claims like "Proposition 8 would force educators to teach gay marriage in schools," "religious people are losing their rights," or "homosexuality is the same as pedophilia and bestiality." For example, national TV news reports cited Bill O'Reilly comparing gay marriage to interspecies marriage (ultimately allowing "for a person to marry a goat, a duck, or a dolphin" [O'Reilly, 2009, May 11]), and Mike Huckabee likened gay couples adopting children to taking in stray dogs (Franke-Ruta, 2010). Rather than weighing the accuracy of the sources and their claims, reporters simply covered it. As Marissa put it, "No matter the legitimacy of the group, they have equal weight in the media. In the press, one quote is worth one quote."

Many of the anti-gay-marriage sources who were given the microphone in this debate framed their opposition, not with credible, logical, or legitimate concerns, but, as Kate described, with the notion that gay and lesbian people are "sick, other, different, icky." As a spokesperson for the leading national lesbian rights organization, she explained, "It could be CNN. It could be MSNBC. It can be the *New York Times* quoting our most virulent enemies, who, if they could deny us oxygen, they'd deny us oxygen. It's not just [about] marriage for them. It's like the existence of gay people is repellent to them. Yet [the press will] still constantly go back to them and have them quoted."

Rather than basing the debate on the more legitimate concerns of expanding marriage rights to same-sex families—like the impact on social services, how schools will respect gay and lesbian parents, or how gay divorces should be structured—opposing sources were typically right-wing, anti-gay extremists whose homophobic perspectives were framed as reasonable arguments. As Kate explained at length, "Who they [news organizations] put up instead are people who essentially say that gay and lesbian people are dangerous. They are predatory. They are a threat. They are to be feared. They are going to undermine core values . . . We shouldn't even have to be in that frame any longer, and I feel like it is an enormous failing—either through sometimes incompetence, but mostly just laziness of the mainstream media—that that's the frame they continue to want to operate in."

As chapter 4 detailed, under the auspices of journalistic balance, reporters felt compelled to interview a fringe opposition group to represent the "other side" despite overwhelming community support for same-sex marriage. Regarding the decision to legalize gay marriages in Iowa, for example, Marissa described a "tidal wave of support" for marriage equality, despite news framing of the "controversy" that cited marginal extremist groups on the far right as credible opposing viewpoints. Informants accused the mainstream media as being an "echo chamber" for the religious right, repeating falsehoods, lies, and diversions that ate up "huge amounts of airtime," as Evan described, similar to the "death panels" rhetoric in the debate over universal health care (claims that "Obama-care" would pull the life support plug from Grandma).

Even though the oppositional sources in this round were fewer in number, activists pointed out how reporters continued to circulate unfounded and unchecked claims such as "This is about teaching gay marriage in schools," "This will force my church to marry gays," or "Prop 8 proponents are the ones being victimized." News coverage during this time period consistently aired these claims from conservative groups whose ratcheted-up rhetoric made for "good" sound bites. For example, the May 15, 2008, evening newscast of CNN began with a standard shot of cheering, exuberant couples outside the state courthouse following the California Supreme Court decision that would allow them to marry (Doss, 2008, May 15). But as the anchor reminds viewers, "Not everyone is celebrating." An exasperated Randy Thomasson of the Campaign for Children and Families tells reporters, "This is what the California Supreme Court has said: 'Children, you have a new role model: Homosexual marriage. Aspire to it.' This is a disaster!"

In another segment, the June 15, 2008, *CBS Evening News* cites Brian Brown of the National Organization for Marriage, who argued that gay marriage opens the door to polygamy: "You cannot just say, 'Well, why not just two males or two females, why not then three or four?' You've done away with the essential meaning of marriage" (Kaplan, 2008, June 15). ABC's October 31, 2008, evening newscast explains that for evangelicals the Prop 8 outcome is more important than the presidential election. In a glaring instance of circulating vitriolic rhetoric from extremist conservative groups, ABC's Dan Harris narrates, "It would force churches to marry gays, force schools to teach gay marriage, and open the door to pedophilia and bestiality." An unidentified young woman is interviewed who flatly explains, "A person could say 'I'm in love with my dog. Why shouldn't we be married?'" (Banner, 2008, October 31). Similarly, following the California Supreme Court decision to uphold the voter ban, a student protester outside city hall is interviewed by CBS news reporters, arguing, "Homosexual relationships. It's unnatural. It's unproductive. It's detrimental to our society" (Kaplan, 2008, June 15).

SAN FRANCISCO, CA: People from a group called America Forever join others at a rally in front of the California Supreme Court building as arguments are heard for and against Proposition 8 on March 5, 2009, in San Francisco. (Photo by David Paul Morris/Getty Images)

In addition, televised newscasts consistently replayed the most controversial advertisements produced by conservative and religious groups, in essence providing a larger microphone for apocalyptic rhetoric and giving "free airtime" to the anti-gay-marriage campaign. For example, in a split-screen debate between Tony Perkins of the Family Research Council and Jeff Kours of Equality California, CNN's Campbell Brown displays a paid print advertisement put out by Perkins's group. She reads the text of the ad to news audiences: "Beginning Monday, judges are removing the word 'husband' from California marriage certificates. The next step will be to remove the term 'Father' from birth certificates. Enjoy this Father's Day . . . It might be your last" (Doss, 2008, June 15).

Likewise, it was common for news organizations to air the hyperbolic "Gathering Storm" advertisement produced by the National Organization for Marriage. After the gay marriage victories in Vermont and Iowa, the organization funneled $1.5 million into the campaign, mostly for ad buys in conservative districts. "Gathering Storm" featured people framed in a medium shot against a background of dark, ominous clouds swirling behind them, appearing as if a natural disaster was looming. The actors recite the ad's scripted lines one by one:

"There's a storm gathering." "It is dark." "And I'm afraid." The ad became a viral hit and, because of its questionable production values, was commonly spoofed on social media sites like YouTube as well as on sketch comedy programs like *Saturday Night Live*. It was also regularly replayed on national television news programs, part and parcel in the coverage of the Prop 8 campaign. For example, CNN's April 8, 2009, evening news broadcast (Doss, 2009, April 8) uses the ad to discuss the organization's campaign to keep gay marriage illegal in California by making it "dark and scary." They replay several seconds of the ad, then cut to an interview with Freedom to Marry's Evan Wolfson, who calls the ad "phony," "from the zombie-like stares, to the actors reading the cue cards, to the arguments they're making." Airing these ads is "balanced" in the journalistic sense only by giving a gay rights activist the opportunity to respond. Laudable as that is, giving airtime to vitriolic and irrational claims—and calling it journalism—essentially validates these assertions as reasoned arguments worthy of debate. Alternately, advertisements from the marriage equality movement, which were not as controversial or acerbic, hardly ever appeared in news stories.

Citing the most extreme views on the far right often conflated with another struggle for activists: overriding the stock "God vs. gays" framing that dominated mediated discourses about marriage. As chapter 4 highlighted, religious figures have always been standard sources in mainstream coverage of the gay marriage debate. However, the moralistic framing of the issue grew more pronounced leading up to and following Proposition 8, presenting unique challenges for the movement about how to talk about religious values and the LGBT community.

On Religion: Tackling "God vs. Gays" Framing

In interviews conducted in 2010 and 2011, activist informants time and again discussed their struggle to combat the growing "God vs. gays" framing as "the 'go-to' story in the media." This framing device consistently relied on using religious figures as the stand-in "default opposition" on the marriage issue, unwittingly pitting religious sources against gay couples or LGBT activists in the name of journalistic "balance." As Jessica, a national news director, put it, "We've been getting clobbered in the area of faith on TV for years. The loudest voices were getting the microphone." This sourcing pattern gave opponent groups what Rick called "an unchallenged monopoly on issues of faith, flag, and family," which, according to movement leaders, the gay movement had in the past "ceded without a fight in many respects."

Several groups struggled to separate *civil* marriage from *religious* marriage in the public eye in order to duck this very narrowly defined battle over morality altogether. Others sought to make a religious case for gay marriage by inserting more pro-gay religious perspectives into news discourses. The legal battle over civil marriage rights is, of course, secular, unrelated to religious doctrine or practice. But in these larger cultural battles, marriage is rarely conceived of as a secular institution. Other gay rights issues, such as employment nondiscrimination, hate crimes legislation, bullying in schools, AIDS research funding, and military service, are not conflated with religious and moral values in the same way marriage is. Because civil marriage and religious marriage are so intertwined in our culture, the prominent debate in the media was often staged on moralistic grounds, becoming about "forcing churches to marry gay couples," as Michael put it.

In response, representatives of several of the national gay rights organizations I spoke with in 2010 and 2011 had, over the past year or two, hired someone in a full-time, director-level position to run faith-based outreach efforts and messaging campaigns. While several of these organizations had some religious outreach in 2004 and 2005, it was clear that by 2010 they had funneled additional resources into faith-based campaigns or had employed a new, high-ranking staff member to lead these efforts. As Jessica told me, this was a concerted effort on the part of the movement. "We [the Task Force, HRC, GLAD] all have religion directors now . . . It's all about getting progressive voices, coalitions of progressive faith leaders across the country, in news reports, making sure that we muddy the argument of 'God versus gays,' because that is the real story."

The development and growth of these positions highlights how the gay marriage controversy and its onslaught of media attention have pushed the LGBT equality movement to grow in new directions. Getting "beat up" on moralistic arguments in the press over marriage increased the need for these new positions that were charged with reaching out and mending what is typically seen as the "huge gulf" between the gay world and the religious world, as Julie put it. These staff positions are highly sophisticated in packaging pro-gay religious perspectives, reaching out to LGBT faith groups, building coalitions of supportive local and national clergy, and developing a larger "Rolodex" of spokespeople of faith who are willing to speak in favor of same-sex-marriage rights.

As Carisa, a communications strategist who had been working on gay rights issues for more than 20 years, explained, it was important to diversify the list of religious spokespeople in the press. The movement "needed to go beyond the UUs [Universal Unitarians], the UCCs [United Church of Christ followers] and the reform Jews," the only pro-gay religious sources that had appeared in earlier coverage. The movement now had to tell the story of the

Catholic mom who really struggled with her faith to come to terms with her son's homosexuality, for example. It wasn't enough to have the "usual suspects" of pro-gay religious sources anymore; movement leaders had to build a coalition of diverse faith-based organizations that would publicly support marriage equality. As one example, Marissa, who worked on the messaging regarding the Iowa Supreme Court decision legalizing gay marriages in the state, organized an interfaith alliance. Her organization crafted an amicus brief on behalf of people of faith, and more than 150 religious leaders in Iowa signed it to indicate their full support for marriage equality.

It's difficult to tell, of course, if these strategies worked to help combat the "God vs. gays" framing. The research goals and methodologies employed in this book are not designed to prove a cause-effect relationship between activist goals and media coverage. Nevertheless, compared to my previous media analysis, this sample of news stories from 2008 to 2010 indicated a higher likelihood of having supportive religious spokespersons and perspectives cited in news stories. This was almost never the case in coverage from my earlier analysis in 2003–2004. The conversation surrounding faith, religion, and gay rights became more multifaceted.

As one stand-out example, the December 15, 2008, issue of *Newsweek* featured Lisa Miller's controversial cover story titled "The Religious Case for Gay Marriage." Along with its attention-grabbing (if not somewhat sensationalistic) headline, the cover included an image of a Bible with a rainbow bookmark protruding from it. Her piece attacks the "God vs. gays" dualism, arguing, "Opponents of gay marriage often cite Scripture as the foundation of their objections . . . Scripture gives us no good reason why gays and lesbians should not be [civilly and religiously] married—and a number of excellent reasons why they should" (Miller, 2008, p. 29). In that same issue, Lorraine Ali's "Mrs. Kramer vs. Mrs. Kramer" unpacks the patchwork of legal protections for marriage and parenting that have devastating consequences for same-sex families (Ali, 2008, December 5, p. 32). This particular *Newsweek* issue, and several other stories like it, represented more complex, nuanced coverage of issues of faith and family, questioned social conservatives' definition of morals, presented pro-gay religious perspectives in depth, and showcased the maturation of the issue in the press.

Several other news reports cited supportive clergy as sources (see, for example, the June 17, 2008, broadcast of the *CBS Evening News* [Kaplan, 2008, June 17]) and highlighted religious wedding ceremonies of gay couples getting married in a church by a collared minister as opposed to having a quick ceremony in city hall. For example, the October 31, 2008, episode of ABC's evening newscast (Banner, 2008, October 31) highlighted a case in which local clergy in conservative Kern County, California, took over performing same-sex ceremonies after the county clerk refused to do so. Supportive ministers told camera crews that marrying the couples was "the right thing to do."

But the coverage leading up to and surrounding the controversial Proposition 8 measure in California complicated the movement's attempts to highlight pro-gay religious perspectives. Reports focused on how religious organizations had funneled money into the voter initiatives that banned gay marriages in several states, and it was hard to ignore the impact of faith-based organizations in winning the vote. For example, on November 6, 2008, the day after the 2008 presidential election, *NBC Nightly News* attributed two factors to the Prop 8 victory: the preponderance of African American voters and the campaigning by religious groups. Reporters charged that "the huge outpouring of Christian groups raising millions" and a corresponding "avalanche of television ads" led to the passage of Prop 8 (Wallace, 2008, November 6). For the b-roll that accompanied the journalistic narration, TV news crews panned a crowd of hundreds in a stadium who had camped out to support the ban on gay marriages, showing the congregation singing, praying, and swaying with their eyes closed.

These and other reports highlighted religious groups praying en masse for God to "save" marriage. For example, the October 31, 2008, evening edition of ABC news (Banner, 2008, October 31) told the story of Prop 8 as one of religious conflict, arguing that "religious groups are pitted against one another in the Prop 8 battle." The report began with an evangelical church in San Diego known as "The Call" where "dozens of members" were engaged in a 40-day fast, praying around the clock for God to "stop gay marriage." The camera panned the small room where a dozen or so people were screaming, singing, crying, and swaying. The camera focused on one man singing, "Jesus, you are so beautiful," with his eyes shut tightly, his arms outstretched skyward. To highlight religious conflict, the reporter provided the "other side" of the story near the end of the segment, focusing on a "usual suspect" in the progay camp—a Unitarian church "across town." In this part of the segment, a lesbian couple who appeared to be in their late 40s gave news crews a tour of the church they were married in.

One emblematic television news report highlighted how churches had fueled some $31 million into the anti-gay marriage campaign. As b-roll played of a pastor swaying in front of his majority-black congregation, the reporter narrated, "But what could be priceless is the boost the campaign gets every Sunday in church" (Kaplan, 2008, October 30). Likewise, CNN's coverage of Prop 8 the day after its passage featured a graphic illustration of the major campaign fund-raisers, boiling it down to two competing forces: religious groups on the one side, and Hollywood actors on the other. The split graphic represented, on one half of the screen, the "Yes on 8" campaign showing dollar signs and logos from Focus on the Family, the Knights of Columbus, and the Church of Jesus Christ of Latter-Day Saints. The other side, the "No on 8" campaign, featured head shots of Brad Pitt, Steven Spielberg, and Ellen DeGeneres (Doss, 2008, November 6).

As described in this chapter's introduction, news organizations widely reported that the Mormon Church, "normally reluctant" to participate in political campaigns, funneled tens of millions of dollars into the "Yes on 8" campaign. Church leaders reportedly had a letter read out loud in every church in California urging their members to do "all you can" to pass the initiative. Not surprisingly, then, after Prop 8 passed, the conflict-driven frame of angry gay protesters targeting the Mormon Church became a standard storytelling device. As with other social conflict in the news, coverage of the Prop 8 protests were consistently framed "within paradigms of delinquency and disorder" (Parameswaran, 2004, p. 371). And as in the scene described by

LOS ANGELES, CA: Hundreds of supporters of same-sex marriage marched for miles in protest against the Church of Jesus Christ of Latter-Day Saints on November 6, 2008, in Los Angeles. The protest, which began outside the Los Angeles Mormon temple, opposed the massive financial contributions to the Proposition 8 campaign, the voter initiative that passed to make gay marriage illegal. (Photo by David McNew/Getty Images)

LOS ANGELES, CA: Same-sex marriage supporters sit down in Wilshire Boulevard, blocking traffic, to protest against the Church of Jesus Christ of Latter-Day Saints on November 6, 2008. Protests against religious groups in the aftermath of Proposition 8's passage further fueled the stock "God vs. gays" framing in mainstream news coverage. (Photo by David McNew/Getty Images)

CNN's Anderson Cooper that opens this chapter, the most resonant television images and news photographs focused on visually dramatic protests, such as when gay marriage supporters blocked off part of Santa Monica Boulevard in Los Angeles. According to news reports, gay marriage supporters weren't just angry; they were retaliatory, blockading intersections, shouting outside of churches, and launching online campaigns to "blacklist" local businesses that had donated to the "Yes on 8" campaign.

Additionally, national coverage of the Iowa decision that legalized gay marriages in April 2009 presented same-sex nuptials as incompatible with wholesome, American, middle-class family values. Legalizing gay marriage in Iowa represented a "seismic cultural shift," reported CBS's Katie Couric, "in a place so often portrayed as a bastion of mainstream American values" (Kaplan, 2009, April 4). Marissa, who had directed the messaging in Iowa for seven years, discussed how disappointed activists were with the "shock and awe" sensationalized coverage from the national news outlets. This communications director had worked to ensure that the reporters in Iowa's major media markets were connected to and covering individual couples as "human interest" stories, so that those covering the case were personally invested in the decision. Describing how "gay friendly" Iowa is, and the "tidal wave of support" behind the legislative outcome, activists were struck by how the local coverage differed from that of the national media outlets.

Analysis of activist interviews and media texts indicates how the movement is struggling to define and tackle these questions of faith, religion, and values. Activists sought to either steer clear of moralistic arguments or at least diversify religious perspectives on gay issues. However, the journalistic lens repeatedly structured the issue as one of conflicting moral values, focusing on the role of religious organizations in shaping the vote, using religion as a standard frame to explain the gay marriage "setbacks" in 2008 and 2009. Despite increased efforts to muddy the conversation surrounding religion and gay identity, media reports continued to rely on religious spokespersons as "natural" opponents. Further complicating the reporting surrounding Prop 8 in particular was how issues of race and class became entangled with religious framing, positioning communities of color against the gay community.

"Playing the Race Card": Problematic Framing of Race in LGBT Issues

Often conflated with religious values, many activist informants in interviews conducted in 2010 and 2011 discussed the problematic framing of "racial minorities vs. gays" or, more specifically, "blacks vs. gays." While the lack of African American spokespersons and couples of color has always been a concern of movement leaders, as coverage unfolded, my informants expressed an increasing unease that only "rich white guys" symbolized the marriage issue in the media. This concern was a valid one; as chapter 3 highlighted, in 2003 and into 2004 gay marriage in news reports was very narrowly defined in terms of race and class, presented as a whites-only, middle- to upper-class institution. Rick articulated how framing the issue around faith and values led to misunderstandings about communities of color: "Our opponents always talked as if gay people were on one side and people of faith were on the other. Gay people were all a bunch of rich, white atheists and were opposed monolithically by black people of faith. We knew from polling that that was not true . . . We knew from our own relationships and from knowing the city . . . that it was not true, but we had to show it."

The "blacks vs. gays" framing came to a head in national coverage of the 2008 election of President Barack Obama. The "race frame" became a predominant device that journalists relied upon to tell the story of "what happened" in California. In the coverage of the Prop 8 aftermath, news stories consistently reported that race was a major factor, if not *the* major factor, in losing the vote. As the November 5, 2008, *New York Times* reported, "exit polls indicated [the measure was] hurt by the large turnout among black and Hispanic voters drawn to Senator Barack Obama's candidacy" (McKinley & Goodstein, 2008, November 6). Media reports consistently reported the "70 percent figure," crediting the high turnout in African American voters for the passage of Prop 8. In many activists' minds, this "blacks vs. gays" framing constituted an unfair "blame game" that pitted communities of color against the gay community. As Michael put it, if one were watching television news during this time, the story came down to "local church folk," more often than not from the black community, opposing "privileged white gay men."

In mediated discourses, minority groups are presumably always in conflict, competing for the single seat at the main table. Representing the diversity of the community has always been a concern of the gay activist community, but in responding to this problematic framing, activists had to redouble their efforts to show that marriage was not just an issue for "rich homosexuals" who wanted to "play house." Rick, who worked with local and national reporters covering the legalization of gay marriage in the nation's capital, explained:

> The problem is our opponents really trying to play the race card, if you will. It's to their benefit to make marriage equality an issue of white privilege in a majority black city [Washington, D.C]. I think it sort of riles up their base and it makes it feel foreign and different. A lot of the leaders on the anti-marriage side are black ministers who tend to frame it that way. They never include the sort of fact-reality that it is: that a lot of African American same-sex couples are the ones who want to get married in Washington.

Other groups, like GLAAD, developed and distributed materials to combat the inaccuracies in the reporting of the 70 percent figure. Despite these efforts, there was only one news story that I came across from this sample that featured a critical perspective on the exit poll data. On CNN's November 6, 2008, evening newscast, Anderson Cooper assembled a panel of "experts" to "dig deeper" into the impact of race on the Prop 8 vote (Doss, 2008, November 6). Cooper turned to Roland Martin, an African American columnist and political pundit, asking him why so many African Americans voted for the ban on same-sex marriage: "Is this surprising?" Anderson asked. "No," Martin said, explaining, "They see it as a religious issue." Hilary Rosen, a columnist for the *Huffington Post* who also sat on the panel, called the reporting on race inaccurate. "I think it's a mistake to make this about black versus white voters here. When you look at the actual numbers, 86 or 87 percent of Republicans voted for this as opposed to 36 percent of Democrats. The overall numbers of white people, white Republicans, who voted against gay rights more than African Americans did, so I just think it's not a particularly useful blame game" (Doss, 2008, November 6).

Despite this one exception, news framing almost universally centered on communities of color casting votes against gay rights protections, which made it increasingly difficult for LGBT leaders to resonate with civil rights discourses. Some groups started outreach programs in black and Hispanic neighborhoods. Most tried to foreground minority couples in press reports. As Kate explained, having a diverse range of couples for more targeted media outlets became a priority for the movement as a whole. Organizations need to "use media that's targeted to different communities, but make sure that who we're putting forward as spokespeople look like those people and sound like them." In fact, a few of my white male informants avoided being sources in media reports because of this concern, agreeing to appear on television only as a last resort. As Michael told me, "My partner and I did the CNN interview, and I didn't want to do it, because I didn't think that we were the right spokespeople. And it happened to be that we were the only ones available to do it, so we agreed. I think that there was a constant cognizance of the importance of having people of color as spokespeople."

In the coverage of D.C.'s move to legalize gay marriages in March 2010, then, it was important that the first three gay and lesbian couples married were minority couples. Michael, the Human Rights Campaign's communications director, who orchestrated the events, said, "Our local D.C. coverage, particularly on Marriage Day, was just kind of a home run from an LGBT activist perspective. Especially considering that we're a majority African American city, the first three couples were African Americans, locals, just very sort of identifiable folks that you would expect to be your neighbors. They weren't particularly activist-y themselves. They were just couples who were in love who were sealing their commitment."

These couples had had commitment ceremonies earlier but agreed to participate in another ceremony for the sake of media coverage. They were married again before a dozen television cameras, an additional 20 photographers, and CNN, which broadcast their ceremonies live. In addition to hosting the three ceremonies at their headquarters, the Human Rights Campaign paid for the ceremonies and converted the serial weddings into a full-blown media event. As Michael explained:

> We identified these three couples as people who would be willing to be sort of the first couples married. We wanted to be able to provide media with a good story. The three ceremonies were back-to-back in here, so once all of their

WASHINGTON, D.C.: Rocky Galloway (second from left) and Reggie Stanley
(third from left) hold their daughters at the end of their wedding on the first day
same-sex couples were legally allowed to wed under a new law in Washington,
D.C. In March 2010 the District of Columbia became the sixth in the nation to
recognize same-sex marriages. The couple's two daughters (far left and far right)
also attended the wedding. (Photo by Alex Wong/Getty Images)

guests were in and media was positioned, we had sort of one ceremony and
then the next and then the next without anyone leaving. And after that, we did
a media availability out front where the mayor joined them as well as some of
the council members who were instrumental in passing the bill.

As Michael's story indicates, from an activist perspective, the best stories
were the ones featuring "real couples" getting married, even more valuable
if the couples in the stories were from communities of color who could
demonstrate the racial diversity of the LGBT community. As with similar
media coverage from 2003 and 2004, activists continued to push stories
of "real families" talking about their lives and the challenges they faced in
living without marriage equality. However, other movement leaders argued
that featuring gay and lesbian people in media stories, marketing materials,
and advertisements did little to help the cause—and may actually have hurt
it. These internal conflicts over how best to represent pro-gay perspectives
in the media led to debates over whether—and to what extent—gay couples
and their children should be used to gain support from the "moveable
middle."

Taking the "Gay" out of Gay Marriage

Several of my informant interviews in 2010 indicated that the movement was at a crossroads, having fought and lost several bruising battles in 2008 and 2009. Conversations with California activists were especially instructive in unpacking these tensions. The Prop 8 loss was so "demoralizing" largely because it was avoidable; many within the movement said the "No on 8" campaign was, as Molly put it, like "watching a slow train wreck. It was heartbreaking." She continued: "We absolutely could have and should have won Prop 8, and the fact that we didn't slows the entire national movement down and emboldened the bullies in ways that there will be more suffering, needless suffering, caused because we did not answer that call. That is very frustrating."

Central to this fissure is a debate over who should speak on behalf of the community. Who is the most effective messenger for the movement in mediated public discourse? According to my informants, organizers behind the "No on 8" campaign, a coalition of select gay rights groups, conducted focus groups and survey research with target audiences, the "reachable middle." Their research found "overwhelming evidence" that including images of couples and their children in media materials actually diminished support for marriage equality measures. In test advertisements and media stories, gay couples—in particular, male couples shown with babies or young children— "did not poll favorably," according to several of my activists, including Patrick and Elizabeth. Informants told me that focus groups responded more negatively than positively to the inclusion of interracial couples; young male couples with kids; and images of couples touching, kissing, or even holding hands. As one informant explained, these findings were explosive in the activist community, especially considering the movement's strategic focus on couples and families in messaging. "Some of the worst polling is [with] an interracial male couple holding a baby. That's like the worst thing you could possibly put in a commercial, because it's hitting on so many issues. Oh, that was a big, big, big thing [for campaign organizers]: no gay couples with kids where the kids are in any of the images."

Jessica, a media relations professional, admitted that "older lesbian couples polled really well as opposed to two men with a child." Likewise, standard news media images of two men in tuxes, two women in gowns, and long lines of people wrapped outside a courthouse "didn't always do well in focus groups." One informant recalled a training meeting in which a media director showed different versions of advertisements from previous campaigns, highlighting those that were successful and those that failed. The commercials in which couples were shown touching or holding hands, activists were told, "didn't work."

As a result, the coalition group who ran the "No on 8" campaign in California "very purposefully" omitted same-sex couples and their children from the media and marketing materials. Instead of using gay couples, the campaign relied on "straight allies" as spokespersons, including the parents of gay and lesbian people, leaders from diverse communities, and supportive politicians. This campaign strategy continues a long-standing tradition that has long plagued media representations of LGBT communities: relying on non-gays to speak on behalf of gay concerns while silencing, and in this case symbolically erasing from the picture, those who have the most at stake.

The absence of gay people in the California campaign did not go unnoticed by the press. David Jefferson (2008), an editor at *Newsweek* magazine, wrote a very personal editorial in the "Society" section about how the Prop 8 decision had put his marriage to his partner, Jeff, in limbo. In writing about the failings of the marriage equality campaign, he argued that the "No on 8" ads were offensive and disingenuous: "Gay leaders decided the best way to fight Prop 8 was downplay the 'gay angle' so as not to offend the undecideds. That's right: no gay people allowed in commercials defending gay marriage. Instead, we got Sen. Dianne Feinstein and other well-meaning straight folk talking about the danger of eliminated 'fundamental rights' and stretching beyond credulity by comparing the ballot initiative to the internment of Japanese-Americans during World War II" (p. 54).

This strategic decision to, as Davina put it, "de-gay" gay marriage divided the movement. Some groups just wanted to "do what it takes to win elections," as Patrick said. These informants argued that supportive allies—parents of gay couples, supportive clergy, progressive politicians, women of faith, and the like—should stand in as spokespersons for the movement. Non-gay allies as sources are more effective messengers "for many non-gay people," as one activist said, because "it's easier for them to hear from somebody they can relate to, they identify with." Elizabeth explained: "This is going to sound horrible, but if keeping couples out of commercials and the media means we're going to win marriage equality, then [our organization] would probably be like, okay, our goal is to win marriage equality so that these couples can have rights and benefits, not be on TV."

Others in the movement criticized the controversial move that worked to "whitewash" same-sex marriage, arguing that the research was unfounded and that the campaign's removal of gay couples smacked of what Davina called "internalized homophobia." Groups like the Family Equality Council protested the decision, arguing, "We have to convince them [the coalition] that this is not right—that our children should be in these pictures." Another said, "You're so stuck on the polling and the numbers that you're keeping this from being what it really is, which is about gay people and gay couples." As a result, when it came to Question 1 in Maine the following year, organizers went against the "overwhelming evidence" and decidedly inserted gay couples and families back into the campaign messaging, only to lose again. Speaking specifically about an advertisement that featured a lesbian couple and their teenage son, Patrick said, "In Maine [the campaign] essentially said 'f off' to the research and we're going to do it our way. And here we lose again because that campaign was done—and they came close to winning—but that campaign was done to satisfy activists . . . not to actually win."

Understandably, these competing tactics and the ensuing losses forced movement leaders to engage in a series of "uncomfortable conversations." What resulted was an even greater rift between what Molly termed the "grass roots" of the movement, the couples and activists who work outside of the professional gay establishment, and "Gay, Inc.," a select group of elite social actors who work for professional organizations on behalf of the movement. She referred to this tension as a "class divide" between the grassroots members and elite gay organizations. "You [the grass roots] just don't have the same opportunities. You hope that maybe you'll run into a rich, gay donor that's like, 'I really like what you guys are doing and I'm going to write you a check,' but it tends to not happen. They [Gay, Inc.] tend to like their galas and dinners where they get to invite their friends. This is sort of something they get to do as a social [thing], primarily, and secondarily making change in the world."

The central criticisms of the campaign from within the movement went beyond the absence of gay and lesbian people in the actual messaging and campaign materials. My activist informants also discussed the campaign's failure to effectively target messaging to racial and ethnic minorities, like translating materials into Spanish or buying airtime in the heavily Latino-populated Central Valley, the large, flat agricultural area that dominates central California. Molly described her attempt to influence the campaign's executive committee of the value of Latino outreach.

> Why don't we have any support or visibility or media buys in the Central Valley? It's a total moveable place there. Our people out there are at the brunt of the anti-gay hatred, and we need to show up for them when we do these big things. They've got to see us there. They're begging. They're pleading. "Do something." We showed them facts and statistics showing how much cheaper it was to buy there—if you buy Spanish-language, how much cheaper it was. You get so much more bang for your buck. Every different angle we could

think of. Morally, financially, looking at the demographics in the voters and the possibilities. Deaf ears.

Davina went as far as to argue that the exclusion of Latino voters in the campaign was inadvertently racist. "What is it, 40 percent of our population is Latino. Give me a break. And you're not going to do stuff in Spanish? Maddening . . . It was racist."

Movement leaders also cited a failure to call upon and use supportive religious spokespersons because the "No on 8" campaign felt it would be "confusing," effectively pushing away the California Council of Churches, who came forward with clergy wanting to advocate for marriage equality. Several movement leaders told me that in the end the campaign failed to create a compelling message or reason why voters should vote no on Prop 8. Rather than tackling discrimination, the convoluted message was instead, "It's okay if you are unsure about gay marriage," because no matter how you feel, you should still vote no on Prop 8. For example, one ad called "The Conversation" featured two 30-something Caucasian women sitting in their kitchen looking at photographs together:

> WOMAN 1: Here's Bob at the barbeque.
> WOMAN 2: [laughing] Look at his sunburn.
> WOMAN 1: And here's our niece, Maria, and her partner, Julie, at their wedding.
> WOMAN 2: Listen, honestly, I just don't know how I feel about this same-sex-marriage thing.
> WOMAN 1: No, it's okay. And really, I think it's fine if you don't know how you feel. But are you willing to eliminate rights and have our laws treat people differently?
> WOMAN 2: No.
> MALE VOICE-OVER: Don't eliminate marriage for anyone. Vote no on Prop 8.

Citing this example, Davina criticized the campaign for relying on weak language, unclear messaging, and backpedaling. This ad in particular used the label of "partner" over "wife" or "spouse" in a campaign where the movement was trying to distinguish between the limitations of domestic "partnership" benefits and the rights afforded to married couples. Additionally, the campaign defined the issue as "this same-sex-marriage thing," echoing the framing of conservative opposition groups. Too fearful of offending undecideds, the campaign narrowed its political aims to avoid overtly confronting heterosexism and discrimination. The frustration and anger from grass roots movement leaders stemmed from the fact that they had raised the money to fund what was essentially an ineffectual campaign for Gay, Inc. As Davina explained, "[We're] the people who wrote checks to the No on 8 campaign.

We paid for them . . . All our money from our wedding—our real wedding, finally—instead of getting gifts, please write checks, right? So we paid for this kind of airtime."

The loss of marriage rights in 2008 in a progressive area on the "liberal Left Coast" was painful enough, but for many of the movement leaders I spoke with, powerlessly watching the mistakes unfold during the campaign made the loss even more demoralizing. This divide within the movement over media strategies and messaging exemplifies my larger theoretical concerns about the complex relationship between social movements, media discourses, and the possibilities for social change. I turn to these issues in my concluding chapter.

Conclusion: One Step Forward, Two Steps Back

In many ways the evolution of the same-sex-marriage debate in 2008 and 2009 represented the best of times and the worst of times. Additional states were moving forward in legalizing same-sex-marriage rights for gay couples, and more and more people said they supported those rights. In news coverage, stories highlighted an overall "pro-gay" tone in which gay and lesbian perspectives were privileged, opposition groups were granted less of a presence, pro-gay religious and political sources had a stronger voice, and even social conservatives like Laura Bush came out in support of same-sex-marriage rights, which muddied the issue. It was, after all, Ted Olson, a lifelong Republican who served under the Reagan and Bush administrations, who took on the federal case to restore same-sex-marriage rights in California. In a controversial *Newsweek* cover story, titled "The Conservative Case for Gay Marriage" (2008), Olson wrote: "Many of my fellow conservatives have an almost knee-jerk hostility toward gay marriage. This does not make sense, because same-sex unions promote the values conservatives prize. Marriage is one of the basic building blocks of our neighborhoods and our nation . . . The fact that individuals who happen to be gay want to share in this vital social institution is evidence that conservative ideals enjoy widespread acceptance. Conservatives should celebrate this, rather than lament it" (p. 48).

Simultaneously, the media's stock "God vs. gays" and "blacks vs. gays" perspectives problematically dominated the framing of the marriage debate, in particular the Prop 8 coverage. Under the glare of the national media spotlight, and forced into an election year campaign, movement leaders were pressured to fight civil rights battles in a media-centric public sphere. Concerns over controlling the message, appealing to the moveable middle, and winning elections proved exclusionary. Gay and lesbian couples and their families, once central to the movement's messaging strategy, were purpose-fully removed from the campaign, replaced by a cadre of allies who advocated for civil rights on their behalf. Certainly, building a coalition of diverse groups is both laudable and necessary in moving social justice causes forward. But for many in the movement, tempering the debate only avoided confronting discrimination and heterosexism at its core. From the perspective of these activists, erasing gay images and voices not only hurt the campaign for mar-riage equality but also demoralized the movement from within.

These tensions, of course, are not unique to the issue of marriage equality or to the gay rights movement more generally. As Sarah Sobieraj demon-strates in her book *Soundbitten* (2011), in the quest to gain visibility, to reach and move the public through the channels available in a commercial media system, activist organizations have little to gain and much to lose. Her re-search across 50 diverse organizations found that these efforts not only prove ineffectual, but they also come with potentially disastrous consequences for organizational life. Most activist groups fail to attract the media attention they so desperately seek, and their tireless pursuit of these strategies often works to alienate members and stifle internal dialogue. One of the consequences of a "public relations" approach to political discourse is that activist groups tend to approach members as "potential liabilities in need of management, rather than as trusted peers able to make valuable contributions" (Sobieraj, 2011, p. 136). As I consider in my concluding chapter, the movement gained a considerable amount of visibility over the marriage debate, but it also faced external confrontations and internal struggles as a result.

6. Conclusion

The Trouble with Marriage

Marriage cannot be severed from its cultural, religious and natural roots without weakening the good influence of society.
—President George W. Bush, February 25, 2004,
    calling for a federal constitutional amendment
    to define marriage as a one man–one woman union

Our journey is not complete until our gay brothers and sisters are treated like anyone else under the law, for if we are truly created equal, then surely the love we commit to one another must be equal as well.
—President Barack Obama, January 21, 2013, in his second
    inaugural address, arguing that same-sex couples should
    be allowed to marry legally

In the 2000s "the politics of social difference and gay identity" moved to the center stage in mainstream cultural debate (Becker, 2006, p. 219). The intense media coverage surrounding the issue of same-sex marriage, launched by the *Lawrence* decision in June 2003, fueled America's "straight panic" (Becker, 2006; Walters, 2001b). Straight America had come head to head with the politics of heterosexual privilege over the issue of same-sex-marriage rights. At the center of this confrontation was the fear that gay marriage would destabilize traditional heterosexual unions. For example, the March 3, 2004, episode of *CBS Nightly News* (Reiss, 2004, March 3) featured video of a newly married gay couple jubilantly squeezing their three adopted children in a celebratory family embrace. The ominous voice dubbed over the image was that of Bill Frist, the Senate majority leader, who warned television audiences: "The wildfire will begin . . . same-sex marriage is likely to spread to all 50 states in the coming years."

In the eight years since that story aired, Senator Frist's predication did not come to fruition—not by a long shot. However, the movement toward marriage equality seemed to be shifting, some might argue "inevitably," as Iowa and several states in the Northeast made moves to legalize same-sex marriages. National public opinion polls have continued to show growing support for same-sex-marriage rights. On June 24, 2011, New York became the sixth, the largest, and the most visible state to grant legal status to same-sex nuptials. With a 33 to 29 vote, four members of the Republican majority voted with Senate Democrats to sign the marriage bill into law. Senator Mark Grisanti of Buffalo, who had previously campaigned on an anti–gay marriage platform, told his constituents he had "agonized" over the decision before ultimately supporting the bill: "I apologize for those who feel offended. I cannot deny a person, a human being, a taxpayer, a worker, the people of my district and across this state, the State of New York, and those people who make this the great state that it is the same rights that I have with my wife" (Confessore & Barbaro, 2011). One month later nearly 1,000 gay and lesbian couples rushed to be among the first married in New York State.

At the time of this writing, on the heels of the 2012 presidential election, the issue continues to draw controversy, heated political debate, and media headlines. Same-sex-marriage rights were up for public vote in four states in 2012, and in a historic first, voters approved measures that would legalize gay marriage. Three states—Maine, Maryland, and Washington—endorsed same-sex marriage rights, and not through legislation or court rulings as in the past, but this time at the ballot box. As this chapter's opening epigraph recounts, President Obama pressed for equal marriage rights in his 2013 inaugural address. In referencing the 1969 Stonewall riots, he equated the contemporary gay rights movement to the women's movement and the civil rights movement of the 1960s.

Two months later, the U.S. Supreme Court dove into the debate for the first time in ten years, beginning hearings on two significant gay marriage cases. The decisions, released in June of 2013, ruled the federal Defense of Marriage Act unconstitutional (*United States v. Windsor*) and reinstated legal same-sex marriages in California (*Hollingsworth v. Perry*). In covering the historic decisions, news organizations around the globe routinely featured same-sex couples celebrating, oftentimes in a teary embrace, flanked by cheering supporters and pictured with their infants and young children in tow. Nevertheless, while the Supreme Court's DOMA decision extended federal benefits to those same-sex couples already legally married, it left 29 state-wide bans intact. The Supreme Court stopped short of declaring same-sex marriage a constitutional right, and failed to propose any sort of federal solution to the legal patchwork of marriage benefits and exclusions that exist for gay and lesbian families across the U.S.

Over a decade ago social critic Michael Warner (1999) argued in *The Trouble with Normal* that despite (and perhaps because of) our cultural fascination with gay life, the politics of sex, shame, and identity remain very much alive and well. By embracing the normalization of gay and lesbian identity as its ultimate goal, he argues that the modern gay rights movement has become "a project for divorcing homosexuality first from sex and then from politics" (p. 96). Borrowing Warner's axiom, I will frame the insights from this book project around "the trouble with marriage" in three distinct ways: first, how gay marriage represents a troubling confrontation with straight culture; second, how the marriage conversation was troubling for gay rights activists who sought to influence news frames and images; and finally, how media productions of gay marriage are potentially troubling for those gay and lesbian citizens—in particular those bisexual, transgender, and queer citizens—who don't fit the "normative" mold in this new era of visibility.

Trouble for Straight America

In the 2000s same-sex marriage, first and foremost, meant trouble for "straight America." As the opening quotations of this chapter illustrate, as well as countless others cited in news coverage throughout this debate, gay marriage spoke to the growing anxieties felt by a heterosexual culture struggling to hold on to its traditional hierarchies. The marriage conversation in the 2000s emerged from the conditions of the unprecedented gay and lesbian visibility in the 1990s, a time period when, more generally speaking, being mainstream was boring and "safe," and being different was cool and "edgy." Having a gay friend, like having a black friend, became a symbol for neoliberal tolerance. In the media, "being on the margins held a certain cultural allure" (Becker, 2006, p. 10). But what surfaced from the rise of this cool, edgy, gay-themed media environment in the 1990s was a nation "more nervous about the future of Straight America" (p. 5). As Becker argues, "Members of a naïve mainstream (which had long had the empowering luxury of ignoring what it meant to be white, male, straight, etc.) found it harder to assert the universality of their experience. They struggled to make sense of their newly exposed social positions and tried to navigate a culture where racial and gender as well as sexual identities mattered" (2006, p. 4).

Within this shifting social landscape, for many, marriage became the cultural fault line. As chapter 1 details, when it comes to bids for inclusive citizenship and social equality, marriage has been where people have historically drawn the line. This perhaps explains the paradox in public attitudes toward gay rights and gay marriage. The vast majority of Americans now support a wide range of equal protections for gay and lesbian citizens, including domestic partnership benefits, inclusion in military service, equal access to housing, employment nondiscrimination, and even adoption rights. But still only a slight majority favor same-sex-marriage rights. After all, securing marriage as an exclusively *heterosexual* institution ensures that "no matter how socially integrated gays and lesbians become, straight life and love are fundamentally different from and better than gay life and love" (Becker, 2006, p. 217).

The images that came to represent the gay marriage issue in the media—of same-sex couples donned in traditional wedding attire, exchanging rings and vows, kissing passionately, and cheering in celebration—were a central investigative focus of this book. These visuals came to symbolize the paradox of sameness and difference, alluding to traditional norms and at the same time problematizing them. According to Davina, whose story begins this book, her decade-long practice of "running around in wedding garb" with her partner has been met with mixed reactions from onlookers. "People always sort of smile when they see a bride or a happy couple dressed up," she explained. "They get it. It's sort of transformative. So we've always gotten a lot of 'Congratulations!' when people see us. Sometimes people will give you a free meal. People are excited, they're happy, it's a strange thing . . . [But] are we scaring straight people by doing this? And would we get our message across better if we 'beiged' it down a little bit and tried to be less threatening?"

As Davina suggests, these images of gay people all dressed up like straight marrieds represent a troubling confrontation with straight culture, because, for many, gays and lesbians threaten to "dismantle" the institution simply by claiming access to it. Pervasive media images of elated gay and lesbian couples, newly married, lay bare this confrontation. As Becker (2006) argues, "[News] photos of gay men in tuxedos and lesbians in white dresses cited the ubiquitous imagery of heteronormative wedding photographs while simultaneously queering them, producing an unsettling mix of similarity and difference. Unsettling because, like the logic behind and coverage of gay rights issues in general, such photographs worked to simultaneously blur and sharpen the distinctions between gay people and straight people" (p. 218).

In news texts, visual representations that constructed gay marriage as symbolically *similar to* heterosexual marriage contradicted news anchors' oral scripts that pronounced its radical *difference from* traditional marriage. For example, as my analysis of the July 13, 2004, episode of *Nightline* illustrates (Sievers, 2004, July 13), news producers highlighted this sameness and difference by juxtaposing the celebratory ceremonies of straight couples with those of gays and lesbians. All the while, Ted Koppel's voice-over reminded viewers, "That was then, this is now." As Suzanna Walters (2001b) and Ron Becker (2006) have suggested, the media's propensity to represent gay ceremonies as imitations of heterosexual marriages is not unique to news narratives. The various gay and lesbian wedding ceremonies that emerged on entertainment television in the 1990s and 2000s on shows like *Friends*, *Northern Exposure*, and *Roseanne* also mirrored and reproduced heterosexual norms.

These discourses surrounding gay marriage were troubling for straight America not only because they stirred a debate about gays' and lesbians' bid for inclusive citizenship but also because they subjected marriage itself to a microscopic gaze. At a time when marriage in the United States is far more likely to fail than succeed, and men and women are delaying marriage until later into their adult lives or opting out altogether, the institution seems outmoded at best, and at worst growing obsolete. As the late Andy Rooney editorialized on *60 Minutes* (Hewitt, 2004, March 21), politicians' hand-wringing over same-sex marriages seems misplaced. "Most Americans disapprove of gay marriage, but if Congress gets into the marriage business, it better look into all marriages, not just gay ones, because marriage is in big trouble. More than half of all marriages in the United States are ending in divorce these days. There's so many divorces they make the wedding business look ridiculous . . . So forget making gay weddings illegal, Mr. President [George W. Bush]. If you want to make marriage more stable, make divorce illegal."

Our culture's debates about gay marriage carried out in the media therefore reflect and contribute to larger anxieties over an institution that appears to be fragile and falling out of favor. The conversation about marriage rights offers the *possibility* to reconceptualize our narrow heteronormative foundations of marriage and family, one that has been rooted in retrograde ideas about reproduction and hegemonic gender roles. But those gay rights activists fighting for marriage equality in the mainstream media were forced to tread lightly, careful not to (re)define the institution in ways that would challenge traditional notions of what marriage means.

The Trouble for Activists

The marriage debate was also troubling for gay rights activists, those who initially feared battling over marriage rights in an oppositional arena like the commercial news media. Insisting that marriage was not a battle of their choosing, many of my informants argued that it was the mainstream news media and conservative activists who propelled the issue onto the national political agenda. As chapter 2 details, for them, the "m word" was not only dangerous (potentially inciting a conservative backlash) but utterly inconceivable. Ultimately, political and journalistic pressures made talking about marriage unavoidable, and activists pursued the marriage agenda to combat the images and narratives of gay and lesbian life that had marked the community as unambiguously "anti-family."

Debating marriage equality in the mainstream media certainly created new opportunities for activists to "reform" images of gay life and shape public discourse around an important civil rights issue. Marriage gave gay activists "a larger microphone" in which to talk about a wide array of LGBT issues, albeit under the umbrella of relationship recognition. The issue also opened up commercialized spaces in the media and popular culture to new, and in many ways, oppositional representations of gay and lesbian life: lesbian couples donned in white gowns exchanging rings under a flowered canopy, or two fathers burping their newborn son.

For the most part, the "poster couples" who appeared in news stories, the ones handpicked by the activist organizations to represent the issue, were selected to appeal to mainstream news audiences. Visual representations of the community, once centered on urban street life; dark, seedy bars; and leather festivals, were transformed in reports on the marriage issue as gay and lesbian life became domesticated in typically heteronormative ways. Interviews with activists revealed that this was not accidental, but part of an overall media project to win the "battle to be boring," to normalize (or, as critics might argue, "sanitize") gay and lesbian identity for the mainstream. In the battle over images, gay rights activists seem to have met their stated goals of presenting the new face of gay and lesbian citizenship—couples getting married, raising children, or simply walking their dogs in a quiet suburban neighborhood. These narratives persisted across the time span of this study, whether they were the stories of celebrity couples like Rosie and Kelly O'Donnell or the tales of lesser-known private citizens and their families like Carol and Kay, who became part of the media spectacle only because of the cultural fascination with gay marriage.

Additionally, this book has also documented how these marriage battles pushed the movement to grow and expand in new directions. The marriage issue elevated the LGBT community to front-page status, increasing the need for public relations personnel and communications departments. The press attention surrounding gay marriage created a new professional cadre of people who were highly sophisticated in packaging positive media messages and content for the mainstream press. In fifty relatively short years, the gay movement has gone from largely unmentionable in the mainstream press to having a group of highly educated, sophisticated professionals, hired by powerful lobbying organizations, whose sole job it is to manage the presentation of gay issues in the news.

A mere ten years ago my activist informants said they had to fight to get *any* coverage of gay issues. Now organizations compete to have their perspectives dominate in news discourses. Most recently these organizations have added faith and religion directors and outreach programming to more effectively respond to the religious opposition to gay marriage. Paradoxically, conservative efforts to use gay marriage to advance their own political agenda in the end participated in solidifying and professionalizing the public relations efforts of the gay rights movement.

Nevertheless, this book has also demonstrated how doing battle in the media also constrained representations of gay and lesbian identity. The marriage debate caused trouble for activists who struggled to (re)direct the conversation, to "sell" gay marriage to straight America, and craft positive narratives and images about gay and lesbian life. My activist informants, as with most social reformers, found their goals and strategies to be at odds with those of a commercial media industry. In following the standards of journalistic neutrality, the news media cited dichotomous viewpoints on either side of the debate, unwittingly providing a platform for extreme anti-gay opponent groups. Problematic framing devices of "God vs. gays" and "blacks vs. gays," along with standard sourcing patterns in the name of reportorial "balance," limited the debate and created a sounding board for historic homophobic discourses. As Cheryl explained, "If there is a reporter out there who is writing a story about a racial issue, they're not going to go to the Ku Klux Klan to get the opposing view. And yet still, with this [gay marriage] issue, it's okay to go to James Dobson, who thinks that gay people are immoral and evil and intrinsically bad, to get the reaction."

Gay marriage opponents who were selected by reporters and editors to voice an opinion in the news—including most politicians, conservative activists, religious leaders, and black community leaders—equated gay marriage with the demise of the institution, social disorder, pedophilia, and polygamy. Following an unwritten professional code, journalists covering the gay marriage issue continued to grant power and prominence to authoritative sources from the legal, medical, religious, and political communities. By 2008 it was less common to see representatives from the conservative far right as sources, but when they did appear, their use of vitriolic and homophobic language, labels, and stereotypes persisted.

Another challenge for activists working with the news media was in their attempts, often unsuccessful, to bring more secular, nuanced, and ideologically diverse perspectives to the debate. Activists struggled to shift the conversation to one in which religious values were a *part* of the gay voice, not set in opposition to it. My informants often found it difficult to recruit and foreground supportive religious leaders, civil rights leaders, political allies, and gays and lesbians of color as media spokespeople. The same consumerist representations that permeated popular culture also worked to exclude many gay and lesbian citizens of color from the marriage conversation.

Even when groups were able to enlist supportive ministers and clergy as sources, and to organize media events around ceremonies of African American same-sex couples (like in Washington, D.C.), stock journalistic frames of "God vs. gays" and "blacks vs. gays" made these stories more difficult to tell. Activists fought, but found it difficult, to disrupt dominant discourses, disseminated in part by media representations, that insert gayness into a white, wealthy, and cosmopolitan lifestyle.

This book has ultimately been concerned with the politics of media representation and the cultural production of news. As recent scholarly work has demonstrated, over the last several decades gay visibility in the media and coverage of gay issues in the press have progressed at a level unprecedented by other social movements and minority groups. But in reporting on the gay marriage debate, as with all gay issues, these stories were filtered through standard journalistic values, written and produced from a heteronormative vantage point. Furthermore, while the marriage issue afforded visibility to some (largely white, middle-class) gay and lesbian couples, it was closed to many others. Ironically, while more visible, gays and lesbians who appeared in the news were mostly seen but not heard.

Trouble for LGBTQ

In his critique of black popular culture, Stuart Hall (1992) wrote, "what replaces invisibility is a kind of carefully regulated, segregated visibility" (p. 24). As this book has demonstrated, activists on the marriage front produced and employed discourses that softened and normalized gay identity for a heterosexual audience. My informants were ever aware of the gay and lesbian "freak show" that had dominated previous news stories and images, and they sought to separate themselves from the extra legal, circus-like mass weddings that appeared as media spectacle.

As Michael Warner and other social critics have cautioned, the marriage issue might mean trouble for those gay, lesbian, bisexual, transgender, and queer citizens who don't "fit the mold" as defined by the politics of visibility. The trouble with marriage, and the fight for gay marriage in particular, is that it is anchored to a set of power relations that embraces the "politics of shame." Marriage inevitably values heterosexual hierarchies and lifelong monogamous commitment over other forms of loving and nurturing.

The notion of marriage as being the "ticket in" to the exclusive club of social acceptance is illustrated time and again in informant interviews and in media reports. Many of my informants referred to marriage as the "stamp of approval." As Marissa explained, for a gay kid growing up in Iowa today, in a state that recognizes same-sex marriages, it's a fundamentally "different world." Marriage "tends to normalize everything else," she said, making it harder to legislate against gay, lesbian, and even transgender citizens. Winning marriage, in other words, makes it easier to pass an anti-bullying law in Iowa, sign the domestic partner benefits bill in New Jersey, and lobby for transgender protections in New York.

This sentiment is echoed in news discourses as well. Dave Wilson, as a recently married gay man, told *Nightline* audiences in 2004, "Everyone we say we're married to, they look at us and get it right away. We don't have to explain our relationship. We don't have to explain who we are or what we are to each other. They get it" (Sievers, 2004, July 13). This notion of recognition and acceptance that Dave and his partner express is inspiring, and the notion of marriage equality as a stand-in issue for a whole range of civil rights is alluring. But we should question whether gay and lesbian people will be welcomed as full citizens *only if* they adhere to these regulated, segregated forms of visibility—monogamous, middle-class, child-rearing, and, of course, married.

For the most part these representations fit the picture that Michael Warner (1999) painted years ago: "Marriage, in short, would make for good gays—the kind who would not challenge the norms of straight culture, who would not flaunt sexuality, and who would not insist on living differently from ordinary folk" (p. 113). The movement's predominant emphasis on civil rights strategies—and on marriage as *the* civil rights issue—could result in an overall depoliticizing and dilution of gay and lesbian identity. In his article "What's Left of Gay and Lesbian Liberation?" Alan Sears (2005) argues that although many gays and lesbians are on the verge of winning full citizenship rights in Canada, Western Europe, and possibly even the United States, the focus on civil rights in capitalistic democracies "leaves many queers out in the cold. The consolidation of lesbian and gay rights has tended to benefit some more than others. Those who have gained the most are people living in committed couple relationships with good incomes and good jobs, most often white and especially men" (p. 93).

In selling one particular version of gay and lesbian life, the movement risks unintentionally casting other forms of gay identity (*not* being part of a monogamous, married, child-rearing couple) to the margins. In this new era of the visible, these particular narratives and images of newly gay marrieds in the news constrained modes of citizenship. News discourses surrounding gay marriage ended up reinforcing the insider/outsider binary that has historically plagued LGBTQ representations, narrowly positioning particular gay and lesbian "poster couples" and families inside the circle of acceptability and legitimacy, while casting other gay forms of loving and family partnership outside of the circle.

As the battle over marriage rights continues, progress is certainly hard to deny. As a civil rights issue, marriage equality for gay and lesbian citizens is a no-brainer. Marriage in the United States continues to be not only a central legal gateway to equality and protections but also a major organizing tool of social and economic life. Despite the inherent problems in that system, it is unlikely to change anytime soon. To deny gay and lesbian citizens access to that institution, despite its problematic formulations, is fundamentally wrong. For many movement leaders, the debate goes beyond securing marriage rights for a few, but rather becomes, as Evan explained, an "engine for eradicating discrimination and prejudice" on a larger scale.

> Marriage has always been a battleground on which larger questions of what kind of country this is going to be have been contested . . . Whether you want to get married or not, you have a stake in these issues. You have a stake in the right boundary between the individual and the government. You have a stake in the separation of church and state. You have a stake in the equality of the races or the equality of men and women. And gay people are now on this battleground, and it's fit and proper that they are. Because this is where we have, time and time again, contested these large questions.

This emancipatory potential can be fulfilled only if the conversation about marriage, ironically, remains focused on the unmarrieds as well. If not, discourses surrounding same-sex-marriage rights risks inadvertently limiting those gay, lesbian, bisexual, transgendered, and queer people deemed "worthy" of full equality.

Appendix

Studying Gay Marriage in the Media

This project was fundamentally concerned not only with news coverage of the same-sex-marriage issue but also with how social actors involved in electoral and cultural politics attempt to shape stories about their lives and issues. In particular I was interested in the process whereby historically marginalized communities harness the power of mainstream commercial media to reform their images and influence public opinion. Critical to shedding light on this process and its challenges, I conducted 30 in-depth, face-to-face interviews with 24 activists who had become media spokespersons for the gay marriage issue. Because my focus for this project was how the gay marriage debate became largely a mediated issue in public discourse, I also investigated hundreds of print and broadcast news stories across an eight-year time period to uncover the dominant narratives and images that were used to communicate stories about same-sex marriage to news audiences.

I adopted a multi-method research design in order to (1) determine the broad boundaries of media content, (2) interrogate the specific meanings of media representation, and (3) examine the behind-the-scenes activities that shape the cultural production of media content. In a move toward methodological diversity and pluralism—a direction that many scholars have called for (Lindloff & Taylor, 2002; McCeod & Blumler, 1987; Miles & Huberman, 1994; Trumbo, 2004)—I employed multiple methodologies to illuminate different versions of the "reality" under study. Because any single mode of inquiry reveals only "certain dimensions of the symbolic reality," my approach was designed "to avoid the personal bias and superficiality that stem from one narrow probe" (Fortner & Christians, 2003, p. 354). In the following sections I explain how and why I approached this project as I did. The first section describes in detail the interview process, justifies the use of the in-depth interview as a mode of inquiry, discusses the selection of informants, and provides the questions that guided the interviews. The second section details the selection of the news media under study, highlights the criteria that shaped my analysis, and justifies the qualitative and quantitative approaches used in this investigation of news content.

Interviewing Gay Activists

My informants for this project represented the "gay voice" in what was constructed as a two-sided conflict: gay rights organizations in favor of same-sex marriage positioned against conservative activists who opposed it. These were the groups and the media spokespersons who were hand-selected to serve as credible sources by major national news organizations. The informants selected for this project, then, had achieved a sense of cultural capital; their presence and visibility in news stories signified that their opinions and perspectives mattered. These were media and public relations professionals who were in a position to promote their issues, stories, and versions of gay and lesbian identity to the American public.

These interviews with leading gay and lesbian rights activists were characterized by researchers as informant interviews (Lindloff & Taylor, 2002), professionals with extensive experience in their organization or movement who have risen through the ranks and can speak knowledgeably about the organization's goals and strategies. They are "savvy social actors" who often provide the researcher entry into the cultural scene. These gay rights activists were generally middle- to upper-class, highly educated, located in urban centers of political and cultural power, and oftentimes had access to state-based bureaucratic institutions. In addition to being activists, they were attorneys, former senators, media executives, and psychiatrists. While a few of these respondents had other jobs outside of their activist work, most were employed full time at gay rights organizations.

The organizations represented in this study had many important similarities—namely, all were entrenched in the marriage debate (whether or not they chose to be); all had a voice in national mainstream media; and all (except for the local Indianapolis activist) were located in large, urban, "progressive" coastal cities. But these organizations also differed in important ways that distinguished their perspectives, goals, resources, outreach efforts, and strategies. For example, these groups differed based on how they defined their primary role in the gay movement. Some groups were largely legal in focus, such as GLAD or Lambda Legal, whose primary responsibilities were in bringing forth litigation and representing plaintiffs. Some were political interest groups and lobbyists, such as Log Cabin Republicans, the gay political interest group affiliated with the Republican Party, and the Massachusetts Gay and Lesbian Caucus, a group responsible for lobbying legislators and advocating for gay rights bills. Others were defined more by their public education efforts and media messaging, such as Freedom to Marry. Of course, categorizing groups in this way is somewhat artificial, as many of these organizations perform all of these roles; for example, the Human Rights Campaign monitors legislative efforts, crafts media and advertising campaigns, and lobbies Capitol Hill.

Organizations also varied widely in terms of size, organizational structure, financial support, funding, membership, and political access. Some groups, such as Marriage Equality USA, described themselves as more "organic" or "grassroots," single-issue organizations made up mostly of private citizens who desired to marry, with only a handful of professional staff and board members. Others were larger, more bureaucratically structured, formal organizations with a large professional staff (like the Human Rights Campaign). Other groups had formed because marriage movement leaders had left the larger multi-issue organizations to start smaller, more single-focus groups dedicated solely to marriage equality (such as Freedom to Marry). As such, these organizations had varying goals for the LGBT community, different ideas about marriage equality and whether or not the issue should be foregrounded, different strategies for their entry into the public conversation, different personal motivations for working in the movement, and different notions about how best to "sell" gay marriage—in other words, how to make gay marriage palatable for a national news audience. These varying perspectives in turn provided a rich platform for my analysis.

As I indicated earlier, I conducted interviews across two different time periods of intense legal and political activity surrounding same-sex marriage: in 2005 and again in 2010. For the first round of interviews, in 2005, my initial content analysis of television news stories in 2003–2004 revealed a total of 17 activists representing 13 national gay rights organizations. After recording a list of sources from gay rights organizations who were cited in national news stories, and securing approval from my institution's human subject review board, I sent potential informants an email inviting them to participate in the study, outlining its purpose and their role in project. I then followed up by phone, sometimes making several calls, in order to answer any questions they had and set up a specific meeting time that would work with their schedule. The informed consent paperwork was then sent by mail or email to each informant so he or she would have the opportunity to review the paperwork prior to the interview. At the time of the face-to-face interview, the informant was invited to read the document again, ask questions, and sign in the appropriate space indicating whether or not they wished to remain anonymous.

While the majority of the informants I contacted agreed to be interviewed, others did not return my phone calls or respond to my emails. Still others declined. Some indicated they were not available, and others said they were wary of being included in the research project. Those working for legal organizations were the most hesitant to be interviewed, as they were concerned about confidentiality and the risk of offering information that could be used misleadingly. Still others were undoubtedly unlikely to trust an unknown researcher with privileged information about the organization or its efforts. The fact that several refused to be interviewed or did not reply to my repeated requests is not surprising considering that media and public relations professionals tend to have busy work lives and at times inflexible schedules. A few were called away last minute from a scheduled interview with me to attend a press conference or meeting. Considering I had no prior access to or relationship with the activist community—I was a PhD student at the time of the initial interviews, and an associate professor during the second round of interviews—I was overwhelmingly pleased with the level of participation. Of the 17 activist sources cited in the initial round of news stories I analyzed, I was able to interview 11 of them (see list of informants below).

Not surprisingly, it was easier to garner access during the second round of interviews, in 2010, as I already had established a relationship with many of my informants. By this time, as I outlined in the introduction to this book, the terrain had shifted rather significantly. Five additional states and the nation's capital had legalized same-sex marriage since the initial time period of my study, and the tone of news coverage and the shift in public opinion showed increased support for marriage equality. I wanted to return to those same informants I had interviewed in 2005 in order to understand how they made sense of these events and how they would characterize the seemingly growing public and political support. I wanted to understand how their goals and strategies had changed, what their persistent and emergent challenges were, what the stories were that they "pitched" now, and how they evaluated and assessed media coverage to date.

I was able to revisit most of the activist informants from my previous study. In a few cases the original informant was no longer with the organization, but I was able to speak to the individual who replaced that informant and thus had a similar role in the organization. There was only one organization I was unable to follow up with, the Massachusetts Gay and Lesbian Political

Caucus based in Boston, because my informant was out of town at the time of my visit and we were unable to find a convenient time to reschedule.

Additionally, through an analysis of national news coverage from 2008 to 2010, I was able to identify several new voices that had emerged. Not surprisingly, new organizations had formed over that time period and had become major players in the national media scene, organizations like Equality California that formed to defeat Proposition 8. In addition, other legacy organizations like PFLAG that had once been largely inactive on the marriage issue had taken a more forceful stance and became a highly visible national media source. Between May 2010 and January 2011, I again traveled to New York City, Washington, D.C., Boston, and San Francisco to interview these informants. I conducted 19 interviews during this time frame: 8 of these with informants I had interviewed previously (or that informant's "replacement," who filled that same role) and 11 with additional informants who were either new to the debate or who had emerged as visible spokespersons for marriage equality over that five-year period.

As Marianne Paget (1983) writes, "What distinguishes the in-depth interview is that the answers given continuously inform the evolving conversation . . . It collects stories, asides, hesitation, expressions of feeling and spontaneous associations" (as cited in Lindloff & Taylor, 2002, p. 172). Since my aim was to allow social movement actors to characterize a complex relationship with media coverage and reporters, I devised an interview schedule (included in this appendix) to keep the protocol flexible enough to allow for spontaneous discussion and follow-up questions but still ensure that consistent questions were asked of everyone.

Interviews with respondents took place in coffee shops, office buildings, college campuses, and gay bars. Most were one-on-one, individual, face-to-face interviews, with the exception of three that were conducted over the phone. In these instances informants were critical figures who were traveling at the time of my visit, or who were called away for a last-minute press conference, so we had to schedule and talk via phone. All but three of my informants agreed to be taped and identified, although at times some informants specified that certain threads of conversation were "off the record." In addition to recording and transcribing interviews, I took extensive field notes during our conversations. When I wasn't able to audio-record the interview, I took extensive field notes. Interviews ranged in time from 45 minutes to 3 hours, with most interviews lasting between 1 to 1 $^1/_2$ hours.

I began by asking informants how they came to be personally involved as activists in their organizations (see interview schedule in this appendix).

I asked how their organization had come to define marriage equality as a goal and why they thought the issue of gay marriage had become such a hot topic in the media and in our public culture. I also asked them about media strategies—what were the ways they tried to advocate for gay marriage and educate the public about their cause? I wanted to learn more about the specific stories activists used to communicate about the issue and then to evaluate those strategies—which ones were successful and which ones failed?

I also invited activists to evaluate their relationship with the news media and to critique news coverage of their community more generally and the gay marriage issue specifically. I viewed activists as participants "in a cultural conversation in which the media are ongoing participants as well" (Press & Cole, 1999, p. 3). Depending on the conversational flow, I often used media examples of same-sex-marriage coverage to spark dialogue and invite critique. I asked respondents to look at stories and images from news magazines and newspaper articles, because I was interested in activists' responses to media discourses about gay marriage. Finally, I asked them if (and how) their organization had changed in response to the marriage debate. In the second round of interviews, depending on whether or not I had previously interviewed the informant, my focus was on how the issue had evolved over the last several years, how their goals and strategies had changed, what new stories had emerged, and what reporters covering the marriage equality issue had gotten right and what they had gotten wrong.

I personally transcribed the first round of audio-recorded interviews; the second round of interviews was transcribed by a private transcriptionist. All told, the interviews generated a vast amount of data, over 300 pages to analyze. I listened to the interviews and read through the transcriptions several times, at first as independent interviews and eventually in relation to each other. During the interview process, and again upon listening to the recordings and rereading the transcripts, I identified several themes that began to emerge. For example, what first struck me was how most activists discussed marriage equality as an issue they were reluctant to pursue in the news media, which I was not expecting. I also noticed key differences in how activists talked about marriage rights for gay and lesbian couples—some relying on civil rights discourses, others insisting that at the core of the issue was "just love," not equal rights. In analyzing the transcribed interviews, then, I noted how activists framed the issue of gay marriage, the various strategies activists highlighted in working with the press, their successes and challenges—what they thought worked, what they thought failed. These "big ideas" that represented points of similarity and divergence among activists served as the basis of my further interrogation and analysis.

Analyzing News Coverage

As I highlight throughout the book, a major aim of this study was to illuminate how prevalent mainstream media were organizing and structuring dominant meanings of the marriage equality issue. Cultural studies scholars who examine news look at the ways in which "institutions and texts of journalism are embedded within larger symbolic myths and cultural narratives" (Parameswaran, 2006, p. 45). Newsmakers routinely rely on familiar cultural stories and mythical archetypes to structure stories in order to "give meaning to incredible events, to explain that which cannot be explained and to reaffirm values and beliefs, especially when those values and beliefs are challenged" (Lule, 2002, p. 276). As Berkowitz (2005) explains, "As both part of their culture and storytellers for that culture, journalists construct stories through narrative conventions that are culturally resonant for themselves and for their audiences" (p. 608). Through "mining" news texts for meaning, this project sought to uncover the predominant cultural myths and narratives journalists relied upon to construct stories about gay marriage.

To do so, I mostly relied on textual analysis to interrogate the journalistic devices that produced dominant meanings of the controversial issue over time. I used textual analysis to uncover the prevalent frames, sourcing patterns, photographic and graphic images, moving images, voice-over narration, and visual representations of married couples and the LGBT community more broadly. Of particular interest of mine were prominent, large-circulation news magazines and national newspapers, evening news broadcasts on network television, and leading prime-time magazine-format television news programs. As I outlined previously, I analyzed media content across two different time periods in order to capture the major legal and political developments that catapulted the same-sex marriage issue into the mainstream press: 2003–2004 and 2008–2011.

Textual analysis, as defined by Alan McKee (2003), is designed for researchers "who want to understand the ways in which members of various cultures and subcultures make sense of who they are, and of how they fit into the world in which they live" (p. 1). Cultural studies scholars think of texts, whether they be artwork, clothing, films, advertising, television shows, or, in this case, news stories, as the "material traces that are left of the practice of sense-making—the only empirical evidence we have of how other people make sense of the world" (p. 15). In this way the process of mining texts for meaning is like looking for clues and making educated guesses about how groups and cultures make sense of their world (Geertz, 1973). As John Hartley (1992) argues, textual analysis allows researchers to recover and critically analyze the "discursive politics in an 'empirical' form" (p. 29).

This analysis of news texts borrows insights from a body of qualitative inquiry that employs textual analysis to "reveal the ideological lenses through which news institutions filter discourses of gender, race, class and nation" (Parameswaran, 2004, p. 379). This body of knowledge recognizes the importance of *contextual* interpretations: the various cultural, historical, political, and organizational contexts within which news is produced and circulates (Fair, 1996). An analysis of media coverage of the gay marriage issue, for example, must contextualize these news discourses within larger popular culture representations of gay and lesbian identity, the historical role of marriage as a social and political institution, and the legal and political events that pushed the issue to the forefront of cultural debate.

To target these stories, I searched the Lexis-Nexis database for stories about "gay marriage" or "same-sex marriage" during the time period June 2003-January 2005, across multiple media outlets, including television news, news magazines, and newspapers. The programs and publications that I selected for analysis were prominent; appealed to large-scale, mainstream news audiences; and substantially and centrally concerned the gay marriage issue. I removed opinion editorials, which, while interesting, were outside the scope of this study. I also eliminated stories that were only marginally concerned with the issue. For example, if a story covered a presidential candidate's stance on a number of issues, with a brief comment that he "opposes gay marriage but thinks it should be left to the states to decide," that story was eliminated, because it was not substantially about gay marriage. If, however, the story was *centrally* concerned with a candidate's position on gay marriage—specifically, how the issue presents a quandary for his campaign and how the issue is likely to affect his electability—then that story was included. Stories were also eliminated from this initial search if they were very short pieces, usually under 20 seconds for television news or under 400 words for print, and were limited to an anchor voice-over with very little or no visual support and no outside reporting. For the 2003–2004 time period, approximately 28 stories remained that fit the criteria in the prominent national media I was interested in, including top feature or cover stories from national news magazines *Time, Newsweek,* and *U.S. News & World Report*; front-page stories from leading national newspapers like the *New York Times* and the *Washington Post*; and episodes of prime-time television news programs *60 Minutes* and *Nightline* in which the entire 30-minute segment was dedicated to the subject of gay marriage.

In addition, for the 2003–2004 time period, these categories uncovered in the textual analysis were used to design the coding instrument for a content analysis, which sought to test for many of these same patterns across a broader universe of news stories—namely, the 93 stories centrally concerned about gay marriage that appeared on NBC, CBS, and ABC evening newscasts between June 2003 and January 2005. While textual analysis was designed to allow for a close reading of several dozen lengthy, in-depth news narratives, the content analysis was designed to uncover broad patterns over time across a larger universe of network news stories. I designed a coding instrument to systematically capture the ways in which broadcast news entities framed the issue of same-sex marriage, privileged particular sources over others, and depicted gay and lesbian couples and their ceremonies. Three units of analysis were selected for coding: each individual news story, each source that was cited in a story about gay marriage, and each gay or lesbian couple/family who was the primary focus of a camera shot.

In its classic conceptualization, "content analysis is a research technique for the objective, systematic and quantitative description of the manifest content of communication" (Berelson, 1971, p. 18). Through critical analysis of these patterns, content analysis provides a powerful tool for researchers to investigate the "big ideas" that shape cultural meanings, "the contours of the ideological environment" (Thomas, 1994, p. 689). Like textual analysis, content analysis is a tool used to make inferences about the symbolic meanings of texts. But unlike textual analysis, content analysis carries the requirement that it be *replicable* (Krippendorff, 1980, p. 21). In other words, there are explicit rules that govern the analysis of the content. Different researchers (in this case, different coders) should be able to apply the same research procedure (the coding instrument) to the same data (television news stories) and produce largely identical results. For the content analysis of television news stories during this time period, the test for intercoder reliability (Krippendorff's alpha) yielded 87 percent agreement for all categories combined.

For the time frame that included January 1, 2008, through March 15, 2010, the same Lexis-Nexis database and search criteria were used to retrieve articles from national print news magazines and national evening television news broadcast transcripts. Analysis included 43 articles from the print edition of national news magazines *Time, Newsweek,* and *U.S. News & World Report* (before it ceased its print product); 20 television news transcripts from network evening news and CNN; and an additional 28 video telecasts of network evening news programs from the Vanderbilt Television News Archive (providing a total of 108 minutes of television news coverage).

Included in the textual analysis of print stories were (1) the photographs and graphic images (with specific attention paid to the racial/gendered/classed identities of news subjects), (2) the captions to the photographs, (3) the story headlines and subheads, and (4) the pull quotes. Additionally, for television news programs, analysis included (5) the moving images that accompanied the voice-over (b-roll), (6) the voice-over narration provided by anchors and reporters (I often followed along using a transcript), and (7) the graphic images and taglines used to title the segment.

I conducted a longitudinal examination of the news coverage to detect the predominant themes, frames, tones, and images that emerged. As Berkowitz (2005) notes, seeing these recurring journalistic devices across multiple media outlets points to their widespread use on the part of mainstream news organizations. I began by performing a careful and close initial reading of each news story to determine the dominant themes and images, taking detailed notes. As patterns in content began to emerge, areas of inquiry about media coverage surfaced, which in turn drove the research questions for this project. For example, why are there more stories and pictures about lesbian couples than gay male couples? Why do certain reoccurring graphics and visual images dominate in television news segments, such as same-sex-figurine wedding-cake toppers? When we as television viewers get to "meet" a gay or lesbian couple, why are they almost always interviewed in their kitchen or dining room? I then read and reread, watched and rewatched, the same stories and segments multiple times to further flesh out the patterns that were emerging. I also paid special attention to the stories and images that seemed to disrupt dominant thematic trends.

I took detailed notes during these multiple viewings and readings, and these notes were eventually categorized and subcategorized into broad areas for further analysis. For example, a section on "Protests" included notes on how these stories showed the clash between gay rights and conservative protesters; "Couples/Families" included notes on the gay and lesbian couples and their children that appeared in news stories; "Ceremonies" included notes on the same-sex weddings shown in the news; and so forth. Based on critical perspectives from cultural studies and media studies about the emergence of groups from the margins to the mainstream, these images, narratives, and journalistic devices were analyzed and unpacked for their larger cultural significance.

Organizations Interviewed

Equality California (founded 2007), statewide LGBT rights advocacy organization, San Francisco/Los Angeles, CA.

Family Equality Council (founded 1979), national LGBT family advocacy organization, Boston, MA.

Freedom to Marry (founded 2003), national marriage equality organization, New York, NY.

Gay and Lesbian Activists Alliance (founded 1971), Washington, D.C.–based LGBT rights lobbying organization, Washington, D.C.

Gay and Lesbian Advocates and Defenders (founded 1978), New England–based LGBT litigation and public education organization, Boston, MA.

Gay and Lesbian Alliance Against Defamation (founded 1985), national LGBT media watchdog organization, New York, NY.

Human Rights Campaign (founded 1980), largest national LGBT advocacy and political lobbying organization, Washington, D.C.

Indiana Equality (founded 2003), state-based LGBT rights organization, Indianapolis, IN.

Lambda Legal (founded 1973), LGBT civil rights litigation and education group, New York, NY.

Log Cabin Republicans (founded late 1970s), national gay and lesbian GOP organization, Washington, D.C.

Marriage Equality New York (founded 1993), state-based marriage equality organization, a branch of Marriage Equality USA, New York, NY.

Marriage Equality USA (founded 1998), national public education organization for same-sex-marriage recognition, Oakland, CA.

Massachusetts Gay and Lesbian Caucus (founded 1973), state-based LGBT lobbying organization, Boston, MA.

National Center for Lesbian Rights (founded 1977), national LGBT litigation and policy advocacy organization, San Francisco, CA.

National Gay and Lesbian Task Force (founded 1973), national LGBT rights organization, New York, NY.

Parents, Families and Friends of Lesbians and Gays (founded 1972), national LGBT family/ally advocacy group, Washington, D.C.

Victory Fund (founded 1991), national electoral fund-raising/campaign group supporting out LGBT political candidates, Washington, D.C.

Activists Interviewed

Barron, Christopher. National political director, Log Cabin Republicans. In-person interview, October 2005.

Bashir, Samiya. Communications director, Freedom to Marry. In-person interview, January 2006.

Brown, Elizabeth. Director of policy and programs, PFLAG. In-person interview, June 2010.

Chrisler, Jennifer. Executive director, Family Equality Council. Phone interview, August 2010.

Cole, Michael. Communications coordinator, later press secretary, Human Rights Campaign. In-person interviews, October 2005; June 2010.

Cunningham, Carisa. Director of public affairs and education, GLAD. In-person interviews, November 2005; August 2010.

Dison, Denis. Vice president of communications, Victory Fund. In-person interview, June 2010.

Hohl, James. Board member, Marriage Equality New York. In-person interview, May 2010.

Isaacson, Arline. Co-chair, Massachusetts Gay and Lesbian Caucus. In-person interview, October 2005.

Jacques, Cheryl. Former president (2004), Human Rights Campaign; founder, Cheryl Jacques.org (2005-present). In-person interviews, October 2005; August 2010.

Kendall, Kate. Executive director, National Center for Lesbian Rights. In-person interview, January 2011.

Kilbourn, Seth. Vice president for the Marriage Project, Human Rights Campaign. In-person interview, October 2005.

Kotulski, Davina. Executive director, Marriage Equality USA. In-person interview, November 2005; January 2011.

McKay, Molly. Former co-director, Marriage Equality California; former Media Director, Marriage Equality USA. In-person interview, January 2011.

Raja, Vaishalee. Communications director, Equality California. Phone interview, January 2011.

Rosendale, Rick. Vice president of political affairs, GLAA. In-person interview, June 2010.

Sammon, Patrick. Former president (2006–2009), Log Cabin Republicans. In-person interview, June 2010.

Sklar, Roberta. Director of communications, National Gay and Lesbian Task Force. In-person interview, January 2006.

St. John, Mark. Spokesperson, Indiana Equality. In-person interview, November 2005.

Note: I also interviewed four informants who wished to keep their identities anonymous. Their perspectives appear under the pseudonyms Marissa Cogan, Jessica Halstead, Julie Ladd, and Dana Robertson.

Interview Guide

I. Issue Evolution
- A. We've certainly seen a great deal of legal and political activity on the issue of same-sex marriage [since we've spoken last, and/or over the past several years].
- B. [If participant needs prompts or clarifications, in the past 8 months 5 states have made moves to legalize same-sex marriage; *Newsweek* magazine recently reported a "gay marriage surge" in growing public support for gay marriage; alongside setbacks in California and Maine in which voters overturned gay marriage rights in those states.]
- C. What do you make of this recent activity? Do you define these movements as largely progress, or as setbacks, or as both? Can you explain why? [or, if previously interviewed in 2005, a good way to open: We last sat down together in 2005 to discuss the same-sex marriage issue. What has changed in the last 5 years, in your mind?]
- D. What are your thoughts on why the issue of same-sex marriage continues to be such a hot-button issue?

II. Goals

A. What would you define as the major goals of your organization? How does the struggle for same-sex-marriage rights fit in?

—or—

B. Same-sex marriage has been an issue of concern for your organization for some time. How would you rank same-sex-marriage rights among the goals of your organization (e.g., a top priority, secondary to other goals, etc.)? Would you say your emphasis or focus on same-sex-marriage rights has altered over the last five years (say, since the 2004 election, since Massachusetts became the first state to legalize marriage for gay couples)? If so, how?

1. [if remained a priority]: Why has marriage remained an important goal of your organization? Why should it be something the LGBT community fights for? What is at stake?

2. [if lessened as a priority]: What were the reasons for this reshuffling of priorities? Why has same-sex marriage diminished in its importance for your organization?

3. [If the first time you have interviewed the respondent/organization, you might also ask]:

At what point did same-sex marriage become an active goal of your organization? (or has it always been?) Can you tell me what was the process involved in defining marriage as a goal? How did you come to decide it was an important goal for your organization?

III. Media Strategies

A. Let's discuss media coverage of the same-sex-marriage issue, and of LGBT issues more broadly.

B. You were contacted for this study because you or your organization has been cited as a source in a prominent, national news story. Tell me a bit of what that process is like. Do you actively seek media coverage, or have you been contacted directly by journalists or reporters, or both? (Get at specifics . . . Can you tell me about the last encounter you had with a journalist? Walk me through that experience.)

C. Most of the calls you field from reporters, do they concern the same-sex-marriage issue? Or a variety of issues? What is the breakdown?

D. What have been some of the ways you have advocated for same-sex-marriage rights in the media? Have your strategies been mostly focused on the local level, or national?

E. Have your strategies changed over the last five years? [specific prompts: Can you tell me about that particular brochure/press release/website/story, walk me through that staged event/protest?]

F. On this issue of same-sex marriage, what is it that you want the American public (or global community, depending) to know or understand?

G. What has been the major story or stories you have tried to tell? What are the ways in which you tried to tell this story? What stories have you tried to tell about the lives of the LGBT community more broadly?

H. What have been some of the challenges you have faced in trying to communicate with journalists/reporters/media organizations on this issue?

I. What media strategies have been most effective? Which ones have been least effective?

IV. Media Representation and Evaluation

A. Do you or your organization track media coverage of the same-sex-marriage issue? What changes or similarities have you noted, comparative to previous coverage (in 2004, surrounding Massachusetts, etc.)? Has the "debate" or controversy in the mainstream media remained consistent, or do you see changes or shifts?

B. Discuss specific examples: for example, in the past two years, *Newsweek* magazine has run two different gay marriage stories as their cover, one titled "The Religious Case for Gay Marriage," the other "The Conservative Case for Gay Marriage." What do you make of this coverage?

C. I'm evaluating mainstream media coverage from 2008 to 2010 (stories that have appeared in national newspapers like *USA Today* and the *New York Times*, major magazine coverage in *Time* and *Newsweek*, and television news broadcasts like the *NBC Nightly News* and *60 Minutes*). Has the media largely gotten this story right? What's missing, if anything?

D. In the news media, how do you think your community has been covered?

V. Issue and Organizational Changes

A. How do you explain or make sense of what seems to be some pretty contradictory impulses regarding the same-sex-marriage issue (as in, many states making moves to legalize but voters blocking when put on the ballot)?

B. Do you feel that you are closer to your marriage goals than you were five years ago, or further from them?

C. What does the future hold for same-sex-marriage rights, and for gay rights more generally?

D. How would you respond to members of your community who argue that there are more pressing issues than marriage?

VI. In Closing

A. Do you have any questions for me?

B. Can I call you if I need clarification on any of these points?

C. Would you like to see a copy of the transcript when it is ready?

Notes

Chapter 1. Gay Marriage in an Era of Media Visibility

1. In the interest of readability, I use imperfect terms to refer to the issue of marriage equality for same-sex couples (phrases like "gay marriage" or "same-sex marriage"). I also take the liberty of using somewhat flawed and overly broad phrases to refer to a diverse identity category like "the gay and lesbian community," or "LGBTQ issues." Synonyms like "activists," "groups," and "organizations" are used to refer to a wide range of gay rights organizations that informed this study.

Chapter 3. "The Marrying Kind"

1. The focus of my analysis here is from June 2003 (beginning with the *Lawrence* decision) continuing through January 2005 (capturing the aftermath of the 2004 ballot initiatives) in order to investigate how mainstream news media represented the events that propelled gay marriage into the cultural-political arena. This 17-month time period captures the major legal and political developments that pushed same-sex marriage to the top of the media and public agendas.

2. Racial diversity is important in LGBT representations, and as the following chapters show, activists were concerned that the only people of color who appeared in gay marriage stories were "attached to" or coupled with a white person.

Chapter 4. Gay Marriage Goes Prime-Time

1. A portion of the quantitative analysis from this chapter appeared in Moscowitz (2010), "Gay marriage in television news: Voice and visual representation in the same-sex marriage debate," *Journal of Broadcasting and Electronic Media*, 54(1): 24–39; available online at http://www.tandfonline.com/doi/full/10.1080/08838150903550360.

Chapter 5. Speaking Out

1. The Lexis-Nexis database was used to retrieve articles from national print news magazines and national evening television news broadcast transcripts that included the phrase "gay marriage" or "same-sex marriage" anywhere in the text of the story. The time frame selected for analysis includes January 1, 2008, through March 15, 2010, capturing the major contemporary developments from this time period.

References

Aarons, L. (2003). The changing coverage of gay, lesbian, bisexual, and transgendered communities. In F. Cropp, C. M. Frisby & D. Mills (Eds.), *Journalism across cultures*. Ames, IA: Iowa State Press.

Adam, B. D. (2003). The Defense of Marriage Act and American exceptionalism: The "gay marriage" bias in the United States. *Journal of the History of Sexuality, 12*(2), 259–276.

Ali, L. (2008, December 5). Mrs. Kramer vs. Mrs. Kramer. *Newsweek, 32*.

Alwood, E. (1996). *Straight news: Gay men, lesbians, and the news media*. New York, NY: Columbia University Press.

Armour, S. (2004, April 4). Gay marriage debate moves into workplace. *USA Today*, p. A1.

Armstrong, E. A. (2002). *Forging gay identities: Organizing sexuality in San Francisco, 1950–1994*. Chicago, IL: University of Chicago Press.

Baker, P. (2012, September 5). At the democratic convention, an emphasis on social issues. *The caucus: The politics and government blog of the Times*. Retrieved October 10, 2012, from http://thecaucus.blogs.nytimes.com/2012/09/05/at-the-democratic-convention-an-emphasis-on-social-issues.

Banner, J. (Producer). (2008, May 15). Same-sex marriages: Landmark ruling. Brian Rooney, *ABC World News with Charles Gibson* [Television broadcast]. New York, NY: ABC News.

———. (2008, June 15). A closer look: Marriage rights. Laura Marquez, *ABC World News with Charles Gibson* [Television broadcast]. New York, NY: ABC News.

———. (2008, October 31). 50 states in 50 days: Wedding fight. Dan Harris, *ABC World News with Charles Gibson* [Television broadcast]. New York, NY: ABC News.

———. (2008, November 12). Culture divide: Same-sex marriage. Dan Harris, *ABC World News with Charles Gibson* [Television broadcast]. New York, NY: ABC News.

———. (2009, April 3). Gay marriage: Same-sex ruling. Chris Bury, *ABC World News with Charles Gibson* [Television broadcast]. New York, NY: ABC News.

———. (2009, April 19). Internal debate: Can GOP say "I Do" to gay marriage? Rachel Martin, *World News Sunday* [Television broadcast]. New York, NY: ABC News.

———. (2009, May 12). Crowning issue: Social issue. Dan Harris, *ABC World News with Charles Gibson* [Television broadcast]. New York, NY: ABC News.

———. (2009, May 26). Split decision: Marriage ruling. Laura Marquez, *ABC World News with Charles Gibson* [Television broadcast]. New York, NY: ABC News.

———. (2009, November 1). Gay marriage battle: Battle moves to Maine. Stephanie Sy, *World News Sunday* [Television broadcast]. New York, NY: ABC News.

Barnhurst, K. G. (2003). Queer political news: Election-year coverage of the lesbian and gay communities on National Public Radio, 1992–2000. *Journalism, 4*(1), 5–28.

Battles, K., & Hilton-Murrow, W. (2002). Gay characters in conventional spaces: *Will and Grace* and the situation comedy genre. *Critical Studies in Media Communication, 19*(1), 87–106.

Becker, R. (2006). *Gay TV and straight America.* New Brunswick, NJ: Rutgers University Press.

———. (2010, August). Guy love: A queer straight masculinity for a post-closet era? Paper presented at the annual Association for Education in Journalism and Mass Communication, Chicago, IL.

Bellafante, Gina. (2005, May 8). Even in gay circles, the woman wants the ring. *New York Times Sunday Styles* (Sec. 9), p. 1.

Belluck, P. (2004a, May 18). Hundreds of same-sex couples wed in Massachusetts. *New York Times*, pp. A1, A21.

———. (2004b, May 17). Massachusetts arrives at day for gay vows. *New York Times*, pp. A1, A19.

Belluck, P., & Zezima, K. (2004, May 16). Hearts beat fast to opening strains of the gay-wedding march. *New York Times*, p. A22.

Bennet, L. (2000). Fifty years of prejudice in the media. *Gay and Lesbian Review, 7*(2), 30–35.

Bennett, J. A. (2006). Seriality and multicultural dissent in the same-sex marriage debate. *Communication & Critical/Cultural Studies, 3*(2), 141–161.

Berelson, B. (1971). *Content analysis in communication research.* New York, NY: Hafner.

Berkowitz, D. (2005). Suicide bombers as women warriors: Making news through mythical archetypes. *Journalism & Mass Communication Quarterly, 82*(3), 607–622.

Bernstein, M. (1997). Celebration and suppression: The strategic uses of identity by the lesbian and gay movement. *American Journal of Sociology, 103*(3), 531–565.

Blumler, J., & Gurevitch, M. (1995). *The crisis of political communication.* New York, NY: Routledge.

Breslau, K. (2004, May 17). A rising tide, rocking boats: The politics of gay marriage roil Oregon's electoral terrain. *Newsweek*, 34.

Broder, J. (2004, December 9). Groups debate slower strategy on gay rights. *New York Times*, p. A1.

Bronstein, C. (2005). Representing the third wave: Mainstream print media framing of a new feminist movement. *Journalism & Mass Communication Quarterly, 82*(4), 783–803.

Bucy, E. P., & Grabe, M. E. (2007). Taking television seriously: A sound and image bite analysis of presidential campaign coverage, 1992–2004. *Journal of Communication, 57*(4), 652–675.

Calmes, J., & Baker, P. (2012, May 9). Obama says same-sex marriage should be legal. *New York Times* online. Retrieved October 10, 2012, from http://www.nytimes.com/2012/05/10/us/politics/obama-says-same-sex-marriage-should-be-legal.html.

Carroll, W. K., & Ratner, R. S. (1999). Media strategies and political projects: A comparative study of social movements. *Canadian Journal of Sociology, 24*(1), 1–34.

Ciasullo, A. M. (2001). Making her (in)visible: Cultural representations of lesbianism and the lesbian body in the 1990s. *Feminist Studies, 27*(3), 577–608.

Clark, D. (1995). Commodity lesbianism. In C. K. Creekmur & A. Doty (Eds.), *Out in culture: Gays, lesbians, and queer essays on popular culture* (pp. 484–500). Durham, NC: Duke University Press.

Cloud, J. (2009, August 31). Obama's gay problem. *Time*, 23–25.

Confessore, N., & Barbaro, M. (2011, June 24). New York allows same-sex marriage, becoming the largest state to pass law. *New York Times* online. Retrieved December 11, 2012, from http://www.nytimes.com/2011/06/25/nyregion/gay-marriage-approved-by-new-york-senate.html?pagewanted=all.

Coontz, S. (2005). *Marriage, a history.* New York, NY: Viking.

DePasquale, R. (2004, May 17). I do! *Newsweek* web exclusive. Retrieved May 17, 2004, from http://www.newsweek.com.

Doss, D. (Producer). (2008, May 15). *CNN Evening News* [Television broadcast]. Atlanta: CNN.

———. (2008, June 15). *CNN Evening News* [Television broadcast]. Atlanta: CNN.

———. (2008, November 6). *CNN Evening News* [Television broadcast]. Atlanta: CNN.

———. (2009, April 8). *CNN Evening News* [Television broadcast]. Atlanta: CNN.

Dow, B. (2001). Ellen, television, and the politics of gay and lesbian visibility. *Critical Studies in Mass Communications, 18*(2), 123–140.

Entman, R. M. (1992). Blacks in the news: Television, modern racism, and social change. *Journalism Quarterly, 69*(2), 341–361.

Entman, R. M., & Rojecki, A. (1993). Freezing out the public: Elite and media framing of the U.S. anti-nuclear movement. *Political Communication, 10*, 155–173.

Epstein, S. (1996). *Impure science: AIDS, activism and the politics of knowledge.* Berkeley, CA: University of California Press.

Fair, J. E. (1996). The body politic, the bodies of women, and the politics of famine in U.S. television coverage of famine in the horn of Africa. *Journalism & Communication Monographs, 158*, 1–41.

Fejes, F. (2000). Making a gay masculinity. *Critical Studies in Media Communication, 17*(1), 113–117.

Ferree, M. M., Gamson, W. A., Gerhards, J., & Rucht, D. (2002). *Shaping abortion discourse: Democracy and the public sphere in Germany and the United States.* Cambridge, MA: Cambridge University Press.

Fortner, R. S., & Christians, C. (2003). Separating the wheat from chaff in qualitative studies. In G. Stempel III, D. Weaver, & C. Wilhoit (Eds.), *Mass communication research and theory* (pp. 350–361). New York, NY: Allyn & Bacon.

Franke-Ruta, G. (2010, April 12). Huckabee compares same-sex marriage to incest, polygamy. *Washington Post.* Retrieved April 24, 2013, from http://voices.washingtonpost.com/44/2010/04/huckabee-compares-same-sex-mar.html.

Gamson, Joshua (1995/1998). Must identity movements self-destruct? A queer dilemma. In P. M. Nardi & B. E. Schneider (Eds.), *Social perspectives in lesbian and gay studies: A reader.* London, UK: Routledge.

Gamson, W. (1998). Discourse, nuclear power, and collective action. In Philip Smith (Ed.), *The new American cultural sociology* (pp. 230–259). Cambridge, MA: Cambridge University Press.

Gans, H. J. (1979). *Deciding what's news.* New York, NY: Pantheon.

Geertz, C. (1973). Thick description: Toward an interpretive theory of culture. In Clifford Geertz (Ed.), *The Interpretation of Cultures: Selected Essays* (pp. 3–30). New York, NY: Basic Books.

Gilgoff, D. (2003, August 25). Gays force the issue. *U.S. News & World Report,* 12.

———. (2004, March 8). Tied in knots by gay marriage. *U.S. News & World Report,* 28.

Gitlin, T. (1980). *The whole world is watching: Mass media in the making & unmaking of the New Left.* Berkeley, CA: University of California Press.

Goffman, E. (1974). *Frame analysis: An essay on the organization of experience.* London, UK: Harper and Row.

Grabe, M. E. (2000). Narratives of guilt: Television news magazine coverage of the O. J. Simpson criminal trial. *Howard Journal of Communications, 11*(1), 35–48.

———. (2007, May). The liberal bias accusation against journalism: Contradictory evidence from a visual perspective. Paper presented at the International Communication Association, San Francisco, CA.

Grabe, M. E., & Bucy, E. K. (2009). *Image bite politics: News and visual framing of elections.* New York, NY: Oxford University Press.

Grabe, M., & Zhou, S. (1999). Sourcing and reporting in news magazine programs: *60 Minutes* versus *Hard Copy. Journalism & Mass Communication Quarterly, 76*(2), 293–311.

Graber, D. (1997). *Mass media and American politics.* Washington, DC: CQ Press.

Gross, L. P. (2001). *Up from invisibility: Lesbians, gay men, and the media in America.* New York, NY: Columbia University Press.

Gross, L. P., & Woods, J. D. (1999). *The Columbia reader on lesbians and gay men in media, society and politics.* New York, NY: Columbia University Press.

Hall, S. (1992). What is this "black" in "black popular culture"? In G. Dent (Ed.), *Black popular culture* (pp. 21–33). Seattle, WA: Bay Press.

Hartley, J. (1992). *The politics of pictures: The creation of the public in the age of popular media.* New York, NY: Routledge.

———. (1998). Juvenation: News, girls, and power. In C. Carter, G. Branston, & S. Allan (Eds.), *News, gender, and power* (pp. 47–70). New York, NY: Routledge.

Hewitt, D. (Producer). (2004, March 10). Marry me! Same-sex marriage in controversy in San Francisco. Bob Simon, *60 Minutes II* [Television broadcast]. New York, NY: CBS News.

———. (2004, March 21). *60 Minutes* [Television broadcast]. New York, NY: CBS News.

———. (2004, July 13). *CBS Evening News with Dan Rather* [Television broadcast]. New York, NY: CBS News.

Iyengar, S. (1991). Is anyone responsible? How television frames political issues. Chicago, IL: University of Chicago Press.

Jacobs, F. (2004, August 31). TV's gay spin zone. *Advocate,* 72.

Jamieson, K. H., & Capella, J. N. (2000). The role of the press in health care reform debates of 1993–1994. In D. Graber (Ed.), *Media power in politics* (4th ed.) (pp. 327–337). Washington, DC: CQ Press.

Jefferson, D. (2008, November 24). How getting married made me an activist. *Newsweek,* 54.

Jurkowitz, M. (2004, May 19). Gay marriage story drew headlines worldwide. *Boston Globe.* Retrieved May 19, 2004, from http://bostonglobe.com.

Just, M. R., Crigler, A. N., & Buhr, T. (1999). Voice, substance, and cynicism in presidential campaign media. *Political Communication, 16*(1), 25–44.

Kamhawi, R., & Weaver, D. H. (2003). Mass communication research trends from 1980–1999. *Journalism & Mass Communication Quarterly, 80*(1), 7–27.

Kaplan, R. (Producer). (2008, May 15). California gay marriage ban overturned. John Blackstone, *CBS Evening News with Katie Couric* [Television broadcast]. New York, NY: CBS News.

———. (2008, June 15). *CBS Evening News with Katie Couric* [Television broadcast]. New York, NY: CBS News.

———. (2008, June 17). *CBS Evening News with Katie Couric* [Television broadcast]. New York, NY: CBS News.

———. (2008, October 30). *CBS Evening News with Katie Couric* [Television broadcast]. New York, NY: CBS News.

———. (2009, April 4). *CBS Evening News with Katie Couric.* [Television broadcast]. New York, NY: CBS News.

Kates, S. M. (1999). Making the ad perfectly queer: Marketing "normality" to the gay men's community? *Journal of Advertising, 28*(1), 25–37.

Keller, J. R., & Stratyner, L. (Eds.). (2006). *The new queer aesthetic of television: Essays on recent programming.* Jefferson, NC: McFarland.

Kennedy, B. (Producer). (2004, May 16). *ABC World News Tonight* [Television broadcast]. New York, NY: ABC News.

Krippendorff, K. (1980). *Content analysis: An introduction to its methodology.* Beverly Hills, CA: Sage.

Landau, J. (2009). Straightening out (the politics of) same-sex parenting: Representing gay families in US newspapers and photographs. *Critical Studies in Media Communication, 26*(1), 80–100.

Lester, W. (2004, December 13). Reassessing gay rights strategy. *Courier Journal,* p. A9.

Liebler, C. M., Schwartz, J., & Harper, T. (2009). Queer tales of morality: The press, same-sex marriage, and hegemonic framing. *Journal of Communication, 59,* 653–675.

Lindloff, T. R., & Taylor, B. C. (2002). *Qualitative communication research methods.* Thousand Oaks, CA: Sage.

Liptak, A. (2004, November 12). Caution in court for gay rights groups. *New York Times,* p. A16.

Lule, J. (2002). Myth and terror on the editorial page: The *New York Times* responds to September 11, 2001. *Journalism & Mass Communication Quarterly, 79*(2), 275–293.

Mansbridge, J. (1986). *Why we lost the era.* Chicago, IL: University of Chicago Press.

McKee, A. (2003). *Textual analysis: A beginner's guide.* Thousand Oaks, CA: Sage.

McKinley, J., & Goodstein, L. (2008, November 6). Bans in 3 states on gay marriage. *New York Times* online. Retrieved April 22, 2013, from http://www.nytimes.com/2008/11/06/us/politics/06marriage.html?gwh=BCEA601287F0F83B6E4B2AEECFC42E36.

McLeod, D. M. (1995). Communicating deviance: The effects of television news coverage of social protest. *Journal of Broadcasting & Electronic Media, 39*(1), 4–20.

McLeod, J. M., & Blumler, J. G. (1987). The macrosocial level of communication science. In S. H. Chaffee & C. R. Berger (Eds.), *Handbook of communication science* (pp. 271–322). Newbury Park, CA: Sage.

Messaris, P., & Abraham, L. (2001). The role of images in framing news stories. In S. D. Reese, O. H. Gandy, & A. E. Grant (Eds.), *Framing public life* (pp. 215–226). Mahwah, NJ: Lawrence Erlbaum.

Miller, Lisa. (2008, December 5). Our mutual joy. *Newsweek*, 28–32.

Miller, M., & Rosenberg, D. (2004, February 23). Something about Mary: Gay-marriage proponents target the veep's daughter. *Newsweek*, 34.

Miles, M. B., & Huberman, A. M. (1994). *Qualitative data analysis* (2nd ed.). Thousand Oaks, CA: Sage.

Morris III, C. E., & Sloop, J. M. (2006). "What lips these lips have kissed": Refiguring the politics of queer public kissing. *Communication & Critical/Cultural Studies, 3*(1), 1–26.

Moscowitz, L. (2010). Gay marriage in television news: Voice and visual representation in the same-sex marriage debate. *Journal of Broadcasting & Electronic Media, 54*(1): 24–39.

Mosvick, M. (2004, March 12). Something to talk about. *Newsweek*, 1.

Nelson, T., & Kinder, D. (1996). Issue frames and group-centrism in American public opinion. *Journal of Politics, 58*, 1055–1178.

Olson, Ted. (2008, January 18). The conservative case for gay marriage. *Newsweek*, 48.

O'Reilly, B. (Producer). (2009, May 11). *The O'Reilly Factor* [Television broadcast]. New York, NY: Fox News.

Owens, L. C. (2008). Network news: The role of race in source selection and story topic. *Howard Journal of Communications, 19*(4), 355–370.

Page, S. (2003, December 17). Bush's gay marriage tack risks clash with his base. *USA Today*, p. A1.

Parameswaran, R. E. (2004). Spectacles of gender and globalization: Mapping Miss World's media event space in the news. *Communication Review, 7*(4), 371–406.

———. (2006). Military metaphors, masculine modes, and critical commentary. *Journal of Communication Inquiry, 30*(1), 42–64.

Pew Forum on Religion & Public Life. (2012). Two thirds of democrats now support gay marriage. July 31, 2012. Retrieved April 15, 2013, from http://www.pewforum.org/Politics-and-Elections/2012-opinions-on-for-gay-marriage-unchanged-after-obamas-announcement.aspx.

Pew Research Center for the People & the Press. (2012). More support for gun rights, gay marriage than in 2008 and 2004. April 27, 2012. Retrieved April 15, 2013, from http://www.people-press.org/2012/04/25/more-support-for-gun-rights-gay-marriage-than-in-2008-or-2004.

Poindexter, P. M., Smith, L., & Heider, D. (2003). Race and ethnicity in local television news: Framing, story assignments, and source selections. *Journal of Broadcasting & Electronic Media, 47*(4), 524–536.

Press, A. L., & Cole, E. R. (1999). Speaking of abortion: Television and authority in the lives of women. Chicago, IL: University of Chicago Press.

Reese, S. (2001). Prologue—Framing public life: A bridging model for media research. In S. D. Reese, O. H. Gandy, & A. E. Grant (Eds.), *Framing public life* (pp. 7–31). Mahwah, NJ: Lawrence Erlbaum.

Reiss, J. (Producer). (2004, March 3). *NBC Nightly News with Tom Brokaw* [Television broadcast]. New York, NY: NBC News.

———. (2004, May 16). *NBC Nightly News with Tom Brokaw* [Television broadcast]. New York, NY: NBC News.

Roberts, C. (1975). The presentation of blacks in television network news. *Journalism Quarterly, 52,* 50–55.

Rosenberg, D. (2003, July 7). Breaking up is hard to do. *Newsweek,* 44.

———. (2003, December 8). Amending their ways. *Newsweek,* 40.

———. (2004, September 22). The "Will & Grace" effect. *Newsweek,* 38–42.

Rosenberg, D., & Breslau, K. (2004, November 15). Winning the "values" vote. *Newsweek,* 23.

Rubin, G. (1989). Thinking sex: Notes for a radical theory of the politics of sexuality. In C. Vance (Ed.), *Pleasure and danger: Exploring female sexuality* (pp. 267–319). London, UK: Pandora Press.

Ruggeri, A. (2008, November 3). A quiet fight over gay adoption. *U.S. News & World Report,* 29–30.

St. John, W. (2004, May 18). Despite uncertainties, out-of-staters line up to marry. *New York Times,* p. A21.

Schwartz, J. (2011). Whose voices are heard? Gender, sexual orientation, and newspaper sources. *Sex Roles 64,* 265–275.

Sears, A. (2005). Queer anti-capitalism: What's left of gay and lesbian liberation? *Science and Society 29*(1), 92–112.

Seelye, K. Q., & J. Elder. (2003, December 21). Strong support is found for ban on gay marriage. *New York Times,* p. A1.

Sender, K. (2004). *Business not politics: The making of the gay market.* New York: Columbia University Press.

Sievers, L. (Producer). (2003, July 2). Public vows, private lives: Gay rights in America. *Nightline* [Television broadcast]. New York, NY: ABC News.

———. (2004, February 24). President George W. Bush supports constitutional ban. *Nightline* [Television broadcast]. New York, NY: ABC News.

———. (2004, May 17). Culture wars. Chris Bury, *Nightline* [Television broadcast]. New York, NY: ABC News.

———. (2004, July 13). The marrying kind. Ted Koppel, *Nightline* [Television broadcast]. New York, NY: ABC News.

Sigal, L. V. (1973). *Reporters and officials: The organization and politics of newsmaking.* Berkeley, CA: University of California Press.

Sloan, D. (Producer). (2003, August 15). A time to be gay? Gay themed television not making some people happy. Chris Connolly, *20/20* [Television broadcast]. New York, NY: ABC News.

———. (2005, April 8). *20/20* [Television broadcast]. New York, NY: ABC News.

Snow, D. A., & Benford, R. D. (1988). Ideology, frame resonance, and participation mobilization. *International Social Movement Research, 1,* 197–217.

Sobieraj, S. (2011). *Soundbitten: The perils of media-centered political activism.* New York, NY: New York University Press.

Strassler, K. (2004). Gendered visibilities and the dream of transparency: The Chinese-Indonesian rape debate in post-Suharto Indonesia. *Gender & History, 16*(3), 689–725.

Sullivan, A. (2004). *Same-sex marriage, pro and con: A reader.* New York, NY: Vintage Books.

Thomas, E. (2003, July 7). The war over gay marriage. *Newsweek,* 38–45.

Thomas, S. (1994). Artifactual study in the analysis of culture: A defense of content analysis in a postmodern age. *Communication Research, 21*(6), 683–687.

Trumbo, C. (2004). Research methods in mass communication research: A census of eight journals, 1990–2000. *Journalism & Mass Communication Quarterly 81(2),* 417–436.

Tuchman, G. (1976). Telling stories. *Journal of Communication, 26*(4), 93–97.

Wallace, A. (Producer). (2008, May 15). California legalizes same-sex marriage. Pete Williams, *NBC Nightly News with Brian Williams* [Television broadcast]. New York, NY: NBC News.

———. (2008, June 17). California's gay marriage law seeing boom in business. Chris Jansing, *NBC Nightly News with Brian Williams* [Television broadcast]. New York, NY: NBC News.

———. (2008, November 6). In depth: How state law allowing same-sex marriages in California was overturned. Pete Williams, *NBC Nightly News with Brian Williams* [Television broadcast]. New York, NY: NBC News.

———. (2008, November 9). Protests over same-sex marriage ban continue in California. Chris Jansing, *NBC Nightly News with Brian Williams* [Television broadcast]. New York, NY: NBC News.

———. (2009, May 24). California Supreme Court to rule on gay marriage this week. Miguel Almaguer, *NBC Nightly News with Brian Williams* [Television broadcast]. New York, NY: NBC News.

———. (2009, May 26). California's Supreme Court upholds ban on same-sex marriages. Miguel Almaguer, *NBC Evening News with Brian Williams* [Television broadcast]. New York, NY: NBC News.

———. (2009, October 31). Maine to vote on same-sex marriage. Ron Allen, *NBC Evening News with Brian Williams* [Television broadcast]. New York, NY: NBC News.

Walters, S. (2001a). *All the rage: The story of gay visibility in America.* Chicago, IL: University of Chicago Press.

———. (2001b). Take my domestic partner, please: Gays and marriage in the era of the visible. In M. Bernstein & R. Reimann (Eds.), *Queer families, queer politics: Challenging culture and the state* (pp. 338–357). New York, NY: Columbia University Press.

Warner, M. (1999). *The trouble with normal: Sex, politics, and the ethics of queer life.* New York, NY: Free Press.

Weaver, D. H. (2007). Thoughts on agenda-setting, framing and priming. *Journal of Communication, 57,* 142–147.

Weiss, J. (2000). *To have and to hold: Marriage, the baby boom, and social change.* Chicago, IL: University of Chicago Press.

White, M. (2003, July 7). The editor's desk. *Newsweek,* 6.

Index

LEIGH MOSCOWITZ is an assistant professor of communication at the College of Charleston.

The University of Illinois Press
is a founding member of the
Association of American University Presses.

Composed in 10.5/13 Adobe Minion Pro
by Lisa Connery
at the University of Illinois Press
Manufactured by Thomson-Shore, Inc.

University of Illinois Press
1325 South Oak Street
Champaign, IL 61820-6903
www.press.uillinois.edu